The Complete Meal Prep Crock Pot Cookbook for Beginners

Quick, Healthy & Delicious Crock Pot Recipes for Smart and Busy People

Lewis Grant

CONTENTS

INTRODUCTION

In our day to day busy lives, we often seem to find ourselves in scenarios where we are unable to take out even a minute out of our busy schedule to spend some time with our family and prepare a hearty homemade meal for ourselves!

Instead, we often tend to visit local fast food and junk food joints, knowing that they are slowly crumbling our body from the inside!

This has turned into a very destructive life cycle of human beings that has led to almost 50% of all Americans (according to Center for Disease Control and Prevention) suffering from some form of cardiovascular disease! Not to mention the fact that heart diseases are currently amongst the top reasons for death as well!

Unhealthy food combined with a hectic and frivolous lifestyle, all contribute to increasing the risk factors for heart disease such as body weight, diabetes, alcohol intake and so on.

The good news, however, is that all is not lost just yet!

With each passing day and each new research article, people are becoming more and more health conscious, and are trying to break free from this unhealthy shackle that is consuming our livelihoods.

Thanks to advancements in both technology and culinary, we are blessed with various appliances and techniques that are developed in hopes of making home cooking more accessible and secure.

The Slow Cooker stands on the top of being one of the most accessible appliances in the market at the moment! It's motto is "Dump and Forget", which is pretty much correct!

Most of the recipes found in this book will entail you merely adding the ingredient to your Slow Cooker, setting it up and then forgetting about it! The cooker will take care of the rest. This helps to save a lot of time as well as give you the opportunity to prepare healthy homemade meals regardless of your cooking skills.

And to make things sweeter, I have included some fantastic Meal Prep tips that should help you prepare the Ingredients for your meals beforehand so that you can quickly add them to your pot and enjoy a less stressful life.

Hearty Meal Prep Ideas

The following Meal Prep ideas are just some of the thousands that you will find floating around! Use these ideas to prepare and store the ingredients to your desired recipes beforehand.

Tips for storage options are provided with each recipe. Foods can also be frozen, usually for up for 3 months.

The primary purpose of these is to inspire you and give you a foundation of Meal Prepping.

Make a plan ahead of time: If you have this book in your hands then you are surely an extremely busy person and you are probably looking for a way to incorporate a healthy lifestyle into your hectic routine, right? Well, the first step to that is to prepare a well-organized Meal Plan. The primary purpose of the Meal Plan will be to provide you an approximate outline of the meals that you are going to prepare for the coming week. This will help you to do your shopping early and prepare them accordingly. During the early days, I would recommend that you keep 2 days a week for prepping and the remaining days just for heating up the already prepared meals.

Keep a good supply of mason jars: Mason jars are terrific, not only for storing memories! But also for storing healthy salads! Assuming that you are a good buff, it might be a good idea to prepare your salads ahead of time and store them in mason jars. Make sure to keep the salad dressing at the bottom of the jar to ensure that greens don't get soggy!

Three-way seasoning in one pan: If you want to stick to lean meats such as chicken, then an excellent way to season multiple batches and prepare them beforehand is to keep them in the same container while separating them using aluminum foil. That will allow you to season and cook up to three or more (depending on how many dividers you are using) types of chicken at the same time! Isn't that amazing?

Roast vegetables that require the same time in one batch: When you are preparing large batches of vegetables for cooking, it is smart to go ahead and prepare them depending on how long they take to cook. For example, you can create a batch of rapid cooking vegetables such as mushrooms, asparagus or cherry tomatoes and a batch of slow roasting veggies such as potatoes, cauliflowers, and carrots to minimize time loss and maximize output.

Keep a good supply of sectioned plastic containers: Sectioned containers are an absolute necessity for serious meal prepping savants! These will effortlessly give you enough space to separate every single component of your meal while making sure that you don't mix everything up and create a mess. The separate ingredients would also be straightforward to find and use.

Facts about Glass Containers

- Glass containers are a bit more expensive but are ideal for long-term storage
- Due to their heavy weight, glass containers are not suitable for "on-the-go" eating
- They are easier to clean
- If you are concerned about plastic safety, then these are the ones to go with!

Facts about Plastic Containers

- Easy to carry and lightweight, ideal for individuals who are always on the go
- They are more convenient and come in a wide variety of sizes and shapes
- They are easy to dispose

BREAKFAST

Full-Belly Honey Coconut Porridge

Serving: 8 / Prep Time: 10 minutes / Cook Time: 8 hours

Ingredients:

- 4 cups light coconut milk
- 3 cups apple juice
- 2 ¼ cups coconut flour
- 1 teaspoon ground cinnamon
- ¼ cup honey

Directions:

1. Stir in coconut milk, apple juice, flour, cinnamon and honey.
2. Close the lid and cook on LOW for 8 hours.
3. Once it goes off, open lid and stir.
4. Serve with an additional seasoning of fresh fruits.

Nutrition Values (Per Serving):

Calories: 372, Fat: 14g, Carbohydrates: 56g, Protein: 8g

Meal Prep Tip/Storage Advice: Once the porridge is cooked, let it cool and divide the servings amongst 4 to 8 individual air tight zip bags depending on your preference. Store them in the fridge for 6-8 days or in your freezer for 6 months. Before serving, simply pour the contents in serving bowl and re-heat in your microwave for 3 minutes.

Early Morning Salmon and Spinach Frittata

Serving: 4 / Prep Time: 15 minutes / Cook Time: 8 hours

Ingredients:

- 10 whole eggs
- ¼ cup unsweetened almond milk
- 1 teaspoon garlic powder
- 1 teaspoon orange-chili-garlic sauce (recipe given)
- ½ teaspoon sea salt
- ¼ teaspoon freshly ground black pepper
- 8 ounces smoked salmon, flaked
- 8 ounces shiitake mushrooms, sliced
- 2 cups baby spinach
- Oil for greasing

Directions:

1. Take a large bowl and add eggs, almond milk, orange chili garlic sauce, garlic powder, salt and pepper.
2. Fold in smoked salmon, spinach and mushrooms.
3. Grease the Slow Cooker with oil.
4. Pour the egg mixture in the Slow Cooker.
5. Close lid and cook on LOW for 8 hours.
6. Serve and enjoy!

Nutrition Values (Per Serving):

Calories: 176, Fat: 9g, Carbohydrates: 7g, Protein: 17g

Meal Prep Tip/Storage Advice: Once the frittata is cooked, let it cool and slice it into 4 servings. Store in air tight containers. A large container should be enough to accommodate all servings. Store in the fridge for 3 days or freezer for 3 months. To serve, heat in microwave for 3 minutes and enjoy!

Easy Going Breakfast Casserole

Serving: 4 / Prep Time: 10 minutes / Cook Time: 10 hours

Ingredients:

- 1 pound cooked bacon, chopped
- 1 red onion, diced
- 1 bell pepper, diced
- 1 tablespoon coconut oil
- 2 large yams, grated
- 2 garlic cloves, minced
- 1 cup coconut milk
- 1 teaspoon dill
- 1 pinch of red pepper
- Salt and pepper to taste
- 1 tablespoon ghee
- Avocado for garnish

Directions:

1. Grease your Crock Pot Slow Cooker with 1 tbsp. of coconut oil.
2. In bowl, add in the grated sweet potato and crushed red pepper.
3. Take a skillet and heat 1 tbsp. ghee.
4. Add garlic, pepper and onions and sauté them for about 2 minutes.
5. Layer ⅓ of your grated sweet potatoes, ¼ of your onion mixture, ⅓ of your bacon and repeat the process twice inside the slow cooker.
6. Take a bowl and whisk in coconut milk, eggs and seasoning.
7. Pour the mixture over your layers in the slow cooker.
8. Cook on LOW for 10 hours. Once ready, let cool and cut into rectangles.

Nutrition Values (Per Serving):

Calories: 369, Fat: 23g, Carbohydrates: 17g, Protein: 20g

Meal Prep Tip/Storage Advice: Once the casserole is cooked, slice it into 4 servings and store them in air tight containers. Store in the fridge for 3 days or freezer for 3 months. To serve, heat in microwave for 3 minutes and enjoy! If you want to avoid freezer burn, try storing them in the freezer proof containers such as stainless steels container.

Mesmerizing Vanilla Sweet Potato Porridge

Serving: 5 / Prep Time: 10 minutes / Cook Time: 8 hours

Ingredients:

- 6 sweet potatoes, peeled and cut into 1 inch cubes
- 1 ½ cups light coconut milk
- 1 teaspoon ground cinnamon
- 1 teaspoon ground cardamom
- 1 teaspoon pure vanilla extract
- 1 cup raisins
- Pinch of salt

Directions:

1. Add the sweet potatoes, coconut milk, vanilla, cardamom, cinnamon to your Slow Cooker.
2. Close the lid and cook on LOW for 8 hours.
3. Open the lid and mash the whole mixture with potato masher, then mix well.
4. Stir in raisins, season with salt and serve.

Nutrition Values (Per Serving):

Calories: 317, Fat: 4g, Carbohydrates: 71g, Protein: 4g

Meal Prep Tip/Storage Advice: Once the porridge is cooked, let it cool and divide the servings amongst 4 individual air tight zip bags. Store them in the fridge for 6-8 days or in your freezer for 6 months. Before serving, simply pour the contents in serving bowl and re-heat in your microwave for 3 minutes.

A Nice German Oatmeal

Serving: 3 / Prep Time: 10 minutes / Cook Time: 8 hours

Ingredients:

- 1 cup steel cut oats
- 3 cups water
- 6 ounces coconut milk
- 2 tablespoons cocoa powder
- 1 tablespoon brown sugar
- 1 tablespoon coconut, shredded
- oil for greasing

Directions:

1. Grease the Slow Cooker with oil.
2. Add the listed ingredients to your Crock Pot and stir well to combine.
3. Place the lid and cook on LOW for 8 hours.
4. Divide amongst serving bowls and enjoy!

Nutrition Values (Per Serving):

Calories: 200, Fat: 4g, Carbohydrates: 11g, Protein: 5g

Meal Prep Tip/Storage Advice: Once the porridge is cooked, let it cool and divide the servings amongst 3 individual air tight zip bags. Store them in the fridge for 6-8 days or in your freezer for 6 months. Before serving, simply pour the contents in serving bowl and re-heat in your microwave for 3 minutes.

Very Nutty Banana Oatmeal

Serving: 4 / Prep Time: 15 minutes / Cook Time: 8 hours

Ingredients:

- 1 cup steel cut oats
- 1 ripe banana, mashed
- 2 cups unsweetened almond milk
- 1 cup water
- 1 ½ tablespoons honey
- ½ teaspoon vanilla extract
- ¼ cup almonds, chopped
- 1 teaspoon ground cinnamon
- ¼ teaspoon ground nutmeg
- oil for greasing

Directions:

1. Grease the Slow Cooker with oil.
2. Add the listed ingredients to your Crock Pot slow cooker and stir well to combine.
3. Cover with lid and cook on LOW for 8-9 hours.
4. Serve and enjoy!

Nutrition Values (Per Serving):

Calories: 230, Fat: 7g, Carbohydrates: 40g, Protein: 5g

Meal Prep Tip/Storage Advice: Once the porridge if cooked let it cool and divide the servings amongst 4 individual air tight zip bags depending on your preference. Store them in the fridge for 8 days or in your freezer for 6 months. Before serving, pour the contents in serving bowl and heat in your microwave for 3 minutes.

The Ravishing Denver Omelette

Serving: 3 / Prep Time: 10 minutes / Cook Time: 6 hours

Ingredients:

- 6 large eggs
- 1 tablespoon unsweetened almond milk
- 1 garlic clove, minced
- ½ teaspoon salt
- ¼ teaspoon freshly ground black pepper
- 8 ounces ham, diced
- 2 red/green bell peppers, seeded and diced
- 1 small onion, diced
- ¼ cup tomatoes, diced
- 2 cups shredded low-fat Cheddar cheese

Directions:

1. Coat the Slow Cooker with cooking spray.
2. Take a large bowl and whisk in eggs, milk, almond, garlic, salt and pepper. Mix well.
3. Fold in ham, bell peppers, onions, tomatoes and 1 cup of shredded cheese.
4. Pour the egg mixture into the Slow Cooker.
5. Place the lid and cook on LOW for 6 hours until the eggs are set.
6. Sprinkle with the remaining 1 cup shredded cheese on top.

Nutrition Values (Per Serving):

Calories: 518, Fat: 33g, Carbohydrates: 14g, Protein: 45g

Meal Prep Tip/Storage Advice: To store, let the omelette cool and slice it into 3 servings. Store them in individual air tight zip bags. Can be kept in the fridge for 3 days and freezer for 2 months. Re-heat in your microwave for 2 minutes before serving.

No Crust –Kale Mushroom Quiche

Serving: 6 / Prep Time: 10 minutes / Cook Time: 8 hours

Ingredients:

- 6 large eggs
- 2 tablespoons unsweetened almond milk
- 2 ounces low –fat feta cheese, crumbled
- ¼ cup parmesan cheese, grated
- 1 ½ teaspoons Italian seasoning
- 4 ounces mushrooms, sliced
- 2 cups kale, chopped

Directions:

1. Grease the inner pot of your Slow Cooker generously.
2. Take a large bowl and whisk in eggs, milk, almond, cheese, seasoning and mix.
3. Stir in kale and mushrooms.
4. Pour the mixture into the Slow Cooker and stir.
5. Cover with the lid and cook on LOW for 8 hours.

Nutrition Values (Per Serving):

Calories: 112, Fat: 7g, Carbohydrates: 4g, Protein: 10g

Meal Prep Tip/Storage Advice: Once the quiche is cooked, let cool and slice it into 4 servings. Store in air tight containers. Store in the fridge for 3 days or freezer for 3 months. When ready to serve, heat in microwave for 3 minutes and enjoy! If you want to avoid freezer burn, try storing them in the freezer proof containers such as stainless steels container.

Beef Broccoli Delight

Serving: 4 / Prep Time: 10 minutes / Cook Time: 8 hours

Ingredients:

- 1 ½ pounds beef round steak, cut into 2 by ⅛ inches strips
- 1 cup broccoli, diced
- 2 cups cooked brown rice
- ½ teaspoon red pepper flakes
- 2 teaspoon garlic, minced
- 2 teaspoons olive oil
- 2 tablespoons apple cider vinegar
- 2 tablespoons soy sauce
- 2 tablespoons white wine
- 1 tablespoons arrowroot
- ¼ cup beef broth

Directions:

1. Take a large bowl and mix soy sauce, red pepper flakes, olive oil, garlic, soy sauce, vinegar, white wine, arrowroot, broth.
2. Transfer the mixture to your Slow Cooker.
3. Add in the beef to your Slow Cooker and close the lid.
4. Cook on LOW for 8 hours.
5. Open the lid just 30 minutes before finishing and add the broccoli.
6. Close the lid and let it complete the cooking cycle.
7. Once ready, serve warm with rice.

Nutrition Values (Per Serving):

Calories: 208, Fat: 12g, Carbohydrates: 11g, Protein: 15g

Meal Prep Tip/Storage Advice: Once the meal is cooked, let it cool and divide the among 4 individual air tight containers. Store the meal in the fridge for 6 days and in your freezer for 6 months.

Classic Apple Cinnamon Oatmeal

Serving: 4 / Prep Time: 15 minutes / Cook Time: 8 hours

Ingredients:

- 1 apple, cored, peeled and diced
- 1 cup steel cut oats
- 2 ½ cups unsweetened vanilla almond milk
- 2 tablespoons honey
- ½ teaspoon vanilla extract
- 1 teaspoon ground cinnamon

Directions:

1. Grease the Slow Cooker.
2. Add the above listed ingredients to your Slow Cooker and stir well.
3. Cover with the lid and cook on LOW for 8 hours.
4. Serve and enjoy!

Nutrition Values (Per Serving):

Calories: 126, Fat: 3g, Carbohydrates: 25g, Protein: 3g

Meal Prep Tip/Storage Advice: Once the porridge is cooked, let it cool and divide the servings amongst 4 individual air tight zip bags. Store in the fridge for 8 days or in your freezer for 6 months. Before serving, pour the contents in a serving bowl and heat in your microwave for 3 minutes.

Carrot Zucchini Oatmeal

Serving: 3 / Prep Time: 10 minutes / Cook Time: 8 hours

Ingredients:

- ½ cup steel cut oats
- 1 cup coconut milk
- 1 carrot, grated
- ¼ zucchini, grated
- Pinch of nutmeg
- ½ teaspoon cinnamon powder
- 2 tablespoons brown sugar
- ¼ cup pecans, chopped

Directions:

1. Grease the Slow Cooker.
2. Add oats, zucchini, milk, carrot, nutmeg, cloves, sugar, cinnamon and stir well.
3. Place the lid and cook on LOW for 8 hours.
4. Divide amongst serving bowls and enjoy.

Nutrition Values (Per Serving):

Calories: 200, Fat: 4g, Carbohydrates: 11g, Protein: 5g

Meal Prep Tip/Storage Advice: Once the porridge if cooked let it cool and divide the servings amongst 4 individual air tight zip bags depending on your preference. Store them in the fridge for 6-8 days or in your freezer for 6 months. Before serving, simply pour the contents in serving bowl and re-heat in your microwave for 3 minutes.

Blueberry Walnut "Steel" Oatmeal

Serving: 8 / Prep Time: 5 minutes / Cook Time: 8 hours

Ingredients:

- 2 cups steel cut oats
- 6 cups water
- 2 cups low-fat milk
- 2 cups fresh blueberries
- 1 ripe banana, mashed
- 1 teaspoon vanilla extract
- 2 teaspoons ground cinnamon
- 2 tablespoons brown sugar
- 1 pinch of salt
- ½ cup walnuts, chopped

Directions:

1. Grease the inside of your Slow Cooker.
2. Add oats, milk, water, blueberries, banana, vanilla, brown sugar, cinnamon and salt to your Slow Coker. Stir well to combine.
3. Place the lid and cook on LOW for 8 hours.
4. Serve warm with garnish of chopped walnuts.

Nutrition Values (Per Serving):

Calories: 372, Fat: 14g, Carbohydrates: 56g, Protein: 8g

Meal Prep Tip/Storage Advice: Once the porridge is cooked, let it cool and divide the servings among individual air tight zip bags. Store them in the fridge for 8 days or in your freezer for 6 months. To serve, pour the contents in serving bowls and re-heat in your microwave for 3 minutes.

POULTRY & RED MEAT

Generous Pot Roast

Serving: 4 / Prep Time: 5 minutes / Cook Time: 8 hours

Ingredients:

- 2 pounds of quarter Boneless beef chuck
- 2 cups hot water
- 1 ounce Onion soup mix, dried
- 3 cups onion, chunked
- 5 cups carrots, chunked
- 6 cups Yukon Gold potatoes, peeled and cut into chunks

Directions:

1. Place beef roast to your Slow Cooker.
2. Take a bowl and add hot water, onion soup and mix it well.
3. Transfer the mixture to the beef in your Slow Cooker.
4. Add carrots, potatoes and onions.
5. Close the lid and cook on LOW for 8 hours.
6. Open the lid and serve hot over bread/rice.

Nutrition Values (Per Serving):

Calories: 664, Fat: 28g, Carbohydrates: 12g, Protein: 82g

Meal Prep Tip/Storage Advice: Once the meal is cooked, let it cool and divide the amongst 4 individual air tight containers. Store the meal in the fridge for 6 days and in your freezer for 6 months. If you want to avoid freezer burn, try storing them in the freezer proof containers such as stainless steels container. Re-heat in microwave for 5 minutes before serving.

Juicy Thai Beef

Serving: 4 / Prep Time: 10 minutes / Cook Time: 8 hours

Ingredients:

- 1 ½ pounds Beef roast
- 3 cups carrots, sliced
- ⅓ cups satay peanut sauce
- ⅓ cups canned light coconut milk
- ¼ cup water
- 2 tablespoons Soy Sauce
- ¼ teaspoon salt
- ¼ teaspoon black pepper

Directions:

1. Take a mixing bowl and add pepper, soy sauce, salt, water, coconut milk and satay sauce. Stir well.
2. Place the beef and carrots to your Slow Cooker.
3. Transfer the sauce mixture in the Slow Cooker and stir well.
4. Close the lid and cook on LOW for 8 hours.
5. Open the lid and shed the beef using fork.
6. Serve and enjoy!

Nutrition Values (Per Serving):

Calories: 280, Fat: 12g, Carbohydrates: 12g, Protein: 32g

Meal Prep Tip/Storage Advice: Once the meal is cooked, let it cool and divide among 4 individual air tight containers. Store the meal in the fridge for 6 days and in your freezer for 6 months. If you want to avoid freezer burn, try storing them in the freezer proof containers such as stainless steels container. Re-heat in microwave for 5 minutes before serving.

Delicious Chicken Curry

Serving: 4 / Prep Time: 10 minutes / Cook Time: 10 hours

Ingredients:

- 10 bone-in chicken thighs, skinless
- 1 cup sour cream
- 2 tablespoons curry powder
- 1 onion, chopped
- 1 jar (16 ounces) chunky salsa sauce

Directions:

1. Place chicken thighs to your Slow Cooker.
2. Add in onions, curry powder, salsa over the chicken.
3. Stir and close the lid.
4. Cook on LOW for 10 hours.
5. Once it goes off, open lid and transfer the chicken to a serving platter.
6. Pour sour cream into the sauce (cooking liquid) in your Slow Cooker.
7. Stir well and pour the sauce over the chicken.
8. Serve and enjoy!

Nutrition Values (Per Serving):

Calories: 386, Fat: 20g, Carbohydrates: 17g, Protein: 35g

Meal Prep Tip/Storage Advice: Once the dish is ready, let it cool and divide among 4 individual air tight containers, based on the servings. Since this is primarily a poultry dish, you can store them in the fridge for 4 days and in the freezer for 3 months. When storing in the freezer, try to opt for containers that are specially designed for freezing at low temperatures to avoid freezer burn. Stainless steel containers are a good option. Re-heat the meal in your microwave for 3 minutes before serving.

Creative BBQ Short Ribs

Serving: 3 / Prep Time: 10 minutes / Cook Time: 8 hours

Ingredients:

- 2 beef short ribs, bone in and cut into individual ribs
- Salt and pepper to taste
- ¼ cup beef stock
- ½ cup BBQ sauce
- 1 tablespoon mustard
- 1 tablespoon green onions, chopped

Directions:

1. Place the ribs to your Slow Cooker. Season with salt and pepper.
2. Add in the stock, BBQ sauce and mustard, toss well to coat it.
3. Place the lid and cook on LOW for 8 hours.
4. Once ready, remove the lid and add the green onions.
5. Toss well and serve.

Nutrition Values (Per Serving):

Calories: 284, Fat: 7g, Carbohydrates: 18g, Protein: 20g

Meal Prep Tip/Storage Advice: Once the meal is cooked, let it cool and divide among 4 individual air tight containers. Store the meal in the fridge for 6 days and in your freezer for 6 months. If you want to avoid freezer burn, try storing them in the freezer proof containers such as stainless steels container. Re-heat in microwave for 5 minutes before serving.

Heartwarming Chickens Cacciatore

Serving: 4 / Prep Time: 10 minutes / Cook Time: 6 hours

Ingredients:

- 1 can (15 ounce) crushed tomatoes
- 8 ounces crimini mushrooms, sliced
- 2 red bell peppers, seeded and sliced
- 2 carrots, peeled and chopped
- 1 onion, sliced
- 3 garlic cloves, minced
- ½ cup low sodium chicken broth
- 2 teaspoons dried oregano
- 2 teaspoons dried basil
- 1 teaspoon salt
- 1 teaspoon freshly ground black pepper
- 3 pounds boneless, skinless chicken thighs

Directions:

1. Add in the tomatoes, mushrooms, bell pepper, onion, carrots, garlic, broth and seasoning to your Slow Cooker. Mix well.
2. Add in the chicken and mix again.
3. Place the lid and cook on LOW for 6 hours. Serve and enjoy!

Nutrition Values (Per Serving):

Calories: 396, Fat: 14g, Carbohydrates: 22g, Protein: 42g

Meal Prep Tip/Storage Advice: Once the dish is ready, let it cool and divide among 4 individual air tight containers. Since this is primarily a poultry dish, you can store it in the the fridge for 3 days and in the freezer for 3 months. When storing in the freezer, try to opt for containers that are specially designed for freezing at low temperatures to avoid freezer burn. Stainless steel containers are a good option. Re-heat the meal in your microwave for 3 minutes before serving.

Hearty Meatloaf

Serving: 4 / Prep Time: 10 minutes / Cook Time: 8 hours

Ingredients:

- 1 ½ pounds ground beef
- ½ teaspoon dried sage
- 1 teaspoon salt
- ½ onion, chopped
- ⅔ cup bread crumbs
- ½ cup milk
- 2 eggs, beaten
- Ketchup for serving (optionally)

Directions:

1. Take a mixing bowl and mix in the listed ingredients, except for the ketchup.
2. Form two individual meat loaves using the mixture (should be of same size).
3. Transfer the meat loaves to your Slow Cooker, side by side, and close the lid.
4. Cook on LOW for 8 hours.
5. Once ready, open lid and serve with ketchup (optionally).

Nutrition Values (Per Serving):

Calories: 276, Fat: 19g, Carbohydrates: 7g, Protein: 18g

Meal Prep Tip/Storage Advice: Once the meal is cooked, let it cool and divide among 4 individual air tight containers. Store the meal in the fridge for 6 days and in your freezer for 6 months. If you want to avoid freezer burn, try storing them in the freezer proof containers such as stainless steels container. Re-heat in microwave for 5 minutes before serving.

A Bowl Of Authentic Pork Chili Colorado

Serving: 8 / Prep Time: 10 minutes / Cook Time: 8 hours

Ingredients:

- 3 pounds pork shoulder, cut into 1 inch cubes
- 1 teaspoon garlic powder
- 1 onion, chopped
- 1 teaspoon chipotle chili powder
- 1 tablespoon chili powder
- 1 teaspoon sea salt

Directions:

1. Add the above listed ingredients to your Slow Cooker and gently stir.
2. Close the lid and cook on LOW for 8 hours.
3. Once ready, serve and enjoy!

Nutrition Values (Per Serving):

Calories: 506, Fat: 37g, Carbohydrates: 2g, Protein: 40g

Meal Prep Tip/Storage Advice: Once the meal is cooked, let it cool and divide among 4 individual air tight containers. Store the meal in the fridge for 6 days and in your freezer for 6 months. If you want to avoid freezer burn, try storing them in the freezer proof containers such as stainless steels container. Re-heat in microwave for 5 minutes before serving.

Totally Awesome Turkey Chili

Serving: 6 / Prep Time: 10 minutes / Cook Time: 6-8 hours

Ingredients:

- 1 ½ pounds, ground turkey
- 1 can (15 ounces) red kidney beans, drained and rinsed
- Salt and cayenne pepper, to taste
- 2 (14 ½ ounces) cans, tomatoes, diced and undrained
- 2 tablespoons ground cumin
- 3 tablespoons. Chili powder
- 3 garlic cloves, peeled, minced, ribs removed and chopped
- 1 red bell pepper, seeds and core removed
- 1 onion, peeled and chopped
- 2 cups cooked white/brown rice

Directions:

1. Stir in the turkey, cumin, tomatoes, garlic, chili powder, red bell pepper and onions into your Slow Cooker. Cook on LOW for 6 hours.
2. Open the lid and add the beans, close the lid and cook for 30 minutes more until the bubbles appear on top.
3. Serve with a drizzle of cayenne and salt. Optionally, serve with rice.

Nutrition Values (Per Serving):

Calories: 470, Fat: 14g, Carbohydrates: 50g, Protein: 31g

Meal Prep Tip/Storage Advice: Once the dish is ready, let it cool and divide among 4 individual air tight containers. Store them in the fridge for 3 days and in the freezer for up to 3 months. When storing in the freezer, try to opt for containers that are specially designed for freezing at low temperatures to avoid freezer burn. Stainless steel containers are a good option. Re-heat the meal in your microwave for 3 minutes before serving.

Lovely Chicken Thighs

Serving: 4 / Prep Time: 10 minutes / Cook Time: 6-8 hours

Ingredients:

- 3 pounds boneless chicken thighs, skinless
- 2 tablespoons apple cider vinegar
- ½ cups honey
- 2 teaspoon garlic powder
- 2 teaspoons paprika
- 1 teaspoon chili powder
- 1 teaspoon red pepper flakes
- Balck pepper and salt to taste

Directions:

1. In a bowl and mix in the garlic pepper, chili powder, paprika, red pepper flakes, salt and pepper.
2. Take another bowl and mix in cider vinegar and honey, then set side.
3. Use the seasoning mix to properly coat the chicken thigh.
4. Pour honey, vinegar mix over the chicken.
5. Transfer all to the Slow Cooker and close the lid. Cook on LOW for 8 hours.
6. Once ready, open the lid, drizzle any remaining glaze on top and serve.

Nutrition Values (Per Serving):

Calories: 234, Fat: 15g, Carbohydrates: 17g, Protein: 8g

Meal Prep Tip/Storage Advice: Once the dish is ready, let it cool and divide among 4 individual air tight containers. Store them in the fridge for 3 days and in the freezer for 3 months. When storing in the freezer, try to opt for containers that are specially designed for freezing at low temperatures to avoid freezer burn. Stainless steel containers are a good option. Re-heat the meal in the microwave for 3 minutes before serving.

Turkey and Assorted Root Veggie Collection

Serving: 8 / Prep Time: 15 minutes / Cook Time: 8 hours

Ingredients:

- 8 ounces baby carrots
- 2 fennel bulbs, sliced
- 8 ounces pearl onions
- 8 ounces button mushrooms
- 1 teaspoon dried thyme
- 1 teaspoon dried rosemary
- 1 teaspoon salt
- ¼ teaspoon fresh ground black pepper
- Zest of 1 lemon
- 2 whole turkey breasts, skin on

Directions:

1. Arrange the baby carrots, fennels, onions, mushrooms at the bottom of your Slow Cooker.
2. Take a small bowl and add thyme, salt, rosemary, lemon zest and pepper. Rub the outside of your Turkey with the mixture.
3. Place turkey in Slow Cooker and top with the veggies.
4. Cover and cook on LOW for 8 hours.

Nutrition Values (Per Serving):

Calories: 347, Fat: 3g, Carbohydrates: 10g, Protein: 60g

Meal Prep Tip/Storage Advice: Once the dish is ready, let it cool and divide among 8 individual air tight containers. Store them in the fridge for 3 days and in the freezer for 3 months. When storing in the freezer, try to opt for containers that are specially designed for freezing at low temperatures to avoid freezer burn. Stainless steel containers are a good option. Re-heat the meal in your microwave for 3 minutes before serving.

Ground Beef And Cabbage Casserole

Serving: 6 / Prep Time: 10 minutes / Cook Time: 8 hours

Ingredients:

- ½ cabbage head, roughly sliced
- 1 onion, diced
- 3 garlic cloves, finely chopped
- 1 ½ pound ground beef
- 1 ½ cups crushed tomatoes
- 2 cups cauliflower rice
- 4 tablespoon coconut oil
- 1 heaping tablespoon Italian seasoning
- ½ teaspoon crushed red pepper
- Salt and pepper to taste
- ½ cup fresh parsley, chopped

Directions:

1. Add the listed ingredients to your Slow Cooker, except for the parsley.
2. Give it a good stir and place the lid.
3. Cook on LOW for 8 hours until the beef is tender and well-cooked.
4. Once ready, open the lid and sprinkle with parsley.
5. Serve and enjoy!

Nutrition Values (Per Serving):

Calories: 320, Fat: 18g, Carbohydrates: 0g, Protein: 17g

Meal Prep Tip/Storage Advice: Once the meal is cooked, let it cool and divide among 4 individual air tight containers. Store the meal in the fridge for 6 days and in the freezer for 6 months. If you want to avoid freezer burn, try storing them in the freezer proof containers such as stainless steels container. Re-heat in microwave for 5 minutes before serving.

Straightforward Ground Pork Stew

Serving: 6 / Prep Time: 20 minutes / Cook Time: 8 hours

Ingredients:

- 1 ½ pounds ground pork
- 1 pound cremini mushrooms, quartered
- 8 ounces pearl onions, peeled
- 2 carrots, peeled and sliced
- 1 green bell pepper
- 1 teaspoon ground cumin
- 1 teaspoon ground coriander
- 1 teaspoon garlic powder
- Dash of cayenne pepper
- 2 cans (14 ounces each) tomato sauce
- 1 teaspoon salt

Directions:

1. Crumble the ground pork and add it to your Slow Cooker.
2. Add the remaining ingredients to your Slow Cooker and stir well.
3. Cover with the lid and cook on LOW for 8 hours.
4. Serve and enjoy!

Nutrition Values (Per Serving):

Calories: 247, Fat: 5g, Carbohydrates: 18g, Protein: 34g

Meal Prep Tip/Storage Advice: Once the dish is ready, let it cool and divide among 4 individual air tight zip bags. You can store them in fridge for 3 days and in the freezer for 3 months. When storing in the freezer, try to opt for containers that are specially designed for freezing at low temperatures to avoid freezer burn. Stainless steel containers are a good option. Re-heat the meal in your microwave for 3 minutes before serving.

Tomato and Garlic Chicken Herbs

Serving: 4 / Prep Time: 10 minutes / Cook Time: 6 hours

Ingredients:

- 3 pounds boneless, skinless chicken thighs
- ½ cup low-sodium chicken broth
- 2 cups cherry tomatoes, halved
- 4 garlic cloves, minced
- 2 teaspoons garlic salt
- ¼ teaspoon ground white pepper
- 2 tablespoons fresh basil, chopped
- 2 tablespoons fresh oregano, chopped

Directions:

1. Add the above listed ingredients to your Slow Cooker and give it a good stir.
2. Cover with the lid and cook on LOW for 6 hours.
3. For freshness, you can add the basil and oregano 30 minutes before the cooking cycle is complete (optionally).
4. Serve and enjoy!

Nutrition Values (Per Serving):

Calories: 247, Fat: 5g, Carbohydrates: 18g, Protein: 34g

Meal Prep Tip/Storage Advice: Once the dish is ready, let it cool and divide among 4 individual air tight containers. You can store them in fridge for 3 days and in the freezer for 3 months. When storing in the freezer, try to opt for containers that are specially designed for freezing at low temperatures to avoid freezer burn. Stainless steel containers are a good option. Re-heat the meal in your microwave for 3 minutes before serving.

Teriyaki Chicken

Serving: 6 / Prep Time: 10 minutes / Cook Time: 5 hours

Ingredients:

- 2 pounds whole chicken drumstick
- ⅓ cup teriyaki sauce
- 1 teaspoon sesame seeds
- Salt and pepper to taste

Directions:

1. Season your drumsticks with pepper and salt.
2. Add them to your Slow Cooker and pour the sauce over the drumstick.
3. Cook on LOW for 5 hours.
4. Once ready, remove the meat from the cooker and place it in a heat-proof oven safe dish. Broil for 5 minutes until crispy.
5. Sprinkle with some sesame seeds and serve!

Nutrition Values (Per Serving):

Calories: 430, Fat: 8g, Carbohydrates: 71g, Protein: 22g

Meal Prep Tip/Storage Advice: Once the dish is ready, let it cool and divide among 4 individual air tight containers. You can store them in fridge for 3 days and in the freezer for 3 months. When storing in the freezer, try to opt for containers that are specially designed for freezing at low temperatures to avoid freezer burn. Stainless steel containers are a good option. Re-heat the meal in your microwave for 3 minutes before serving.

Coconut Pork Curry

Serving: 4 / Prep Time: 10 minutes / Cook Time: 4 hours

Ingredients:

- 2 tablespoons coconut oil
- 4 pounds boneless pork shoulder, cut into 2 inch pieces
- Salt and pepper to taste
- 1 large onion, chopped
- 3 tablespoons garlic cloves, minced
- 3 tablespoons ginger, minced
- 1 tablespoon mild curry powder
- 1 tablespoon ground cumin
- ½ teaspoon ground turmeric
- 1 (14 ounce) can of diced tomatoes
- 1 cup unsweetened coconut milk
- 2 cups chicken stock
- Steamed rice, for serving
- Cilantro, green onions for garnish, chopped

Directions:

1. Process and prepare the ingredients accordingly. Take a large sized skillet and heat the coconut oil.
2. Add the pork in batches, brown it and season with a bit of salt and pepper. Transfer to the Slow Cooker.
3. Making sure that there are at least 2 tablespoons of fat in the skillet, add the onion, garlic, ginger, cumin, curry, turmeric and cook on low heat for 5 minutes.
4. Add the mixture to your Slow Cooker and place the lid. Cook on LOW for 4 hours. Once ready, serve over rice and garnish with cilantro and scallions.

Nutrition Values (Per Serving):

Calories: 419, Fat: 29g, Carbohydrates: 8g, Protein: 31g

Meal Prep Tip/Storage Advice: Once the meal is cooked, let it cool and divide among 4 individual air tight containers. Store the meal in fridge for 6 days and in your the freezer for 6 months. If you want to avoid freezer burn, try storing them in the freezer proof containers such as stainless steels container. Re-heat in microwave for 5 minutes before serving.

Star Anise Short Ribs

Serving: 3 / Prep Time: 10 minutes / Cook Time: 6 hours

Ingredients:

- 1 beef short rib
- 2 small red onions, chopped
- 2 garlic cloves, minced
- 1 teaspoon ground ginger
- 2 pieces of star anise

Directions:

1. Process and prepare the ingredients accordingly.
2. Chop the onions and crush the garlic. Place the beef to your Slow Cooker.
3. Stir in the garlic, onion, ginger, star anise on top of the meat.
4. Pour water of about 1 inch depth.
5. Place the lid and cook on LOW for 8 hours.
6. Season and serve with veggies!

Nutrition Values (Per Serving):

Calories: 347, Fat: 30g, Carbohydrates: 5g, Protein: 13g

Meal Prep Tip/Storage Advice: Once the meal is cooked, let it cool and divide among 4 individual air tight containers. Store the meal in fridge for 6 days and in the freezer for 6 months.

Authentic Jerk Chicken

Serving: 4 / Prep Time: 10 minutes / Cook Time: 8 hours

Ingredients:

- 2 sweet potatoes, cubed
- 1 teaspoon garlic powder
- 1 teaspoon onion powder
- 1 teaspoon coconut sugar
- 1 teaspoon salt
- ½ teaspoon ground smoked paprika
- ½ teaspoon ground allspice
- ¼ teaspoon ground cayenne pepper
- ¼ teaspoon freshly ground black pepper
- ¼ teaspoon ground nutmeg
- 1 pinch of ground cinnamon
- 1 whole chicken (cut into parts)

Directions:

1. Arrange the sweet potatoes in your Slow Cooker.
2. Take a small bowl and add garlic powder, onion powder, salt, paprika, coconut sugar, allspice, black pepper, cayenne, nutmeg and cinnamon.
3. Rub the spice mix over the chicken pieces.
4. Arrange pieces in Slow Cooker on top of the potatoes.
5. Place the lid and cook on LOW for 8 hours.
6. Serve and enjoy!

Nutrition Values (Per Serving):

Calories: 315, Fat: 4g, Carbohydrates: 34g, Protein: 25g

Meal Prep Tip/Storage Advice: Once the dish is ready, let it cool and divide among 4 individual air tight containers. You can store them in fridge for 3 days and in the freezer for 3 months. When storing in the freezer, try to opt for containers that are specially designed for freezing at low temperatures to avoid freezer burn. Stainless steel containers are a good option. Re-heat the meal in your microwave for 3 minutes before serving.

Gorgeous Pepper Steaks

Serving: 4 / Prep Time: 10 minutes / Cook Time: 6 hours

Ingredients:

- 2 pounds beef round steak, sliced against grain
- Salt and pepper to taste
- 1 garlic clove, minced
- ½ onion, sliced
- 1 teaspoon sugar
- ¼ cup soy sauce
- 1 green pepper sliced
- 1 can crushed tomatoes

Directions:

1. Take a bowl and add the above listed ingredients.
2. Mix well and transfer the contents to your Slow Cooker.
3. Close the lid and cook on LOW for 6 hours.
4. Once ready, open lid, transfer to serving platter and enjoy!

Nutrition Values (Per Serving):

Calories: 518, Fat: 45g, Carbohydrates: 2g, Protein: 37g

Meal Prep Tip/Storage Advice: Once the meal is cooked, let it cool and divide among 4 individual air tight containers. Store the meal in fridge for 6 days and in the freezer for 6 months. If you want to avoid freezer burn, try storing them in the freezer proof containers such as stainless steels container. Re-heat in microwave for 5 minutes before serving.

Garlic And Citrus Potato Chicken

Serving: 4 / Prep Time: 10 minutes / Cook Time: 6 hours

Ingredients:

- 1 onion, sliced
- 1 pound red potatoes, diced
- 2 pounds boneless, skinless chicken thighs
- ⅓ cup freshly squeezed lime juice
- ¼ cup freshly squeezed orange juice
- 2 tablespoons extra virgin olive oil
- 7 garlic cloves, minced
- 1 teaspoon salt
- 1 teaspoon dried oregano
- ¼ teaspoon ground cumin
- 1 lemon, sliced
- 1 jalapeno, seeded and sliced

Directions:

1. Place the onion and potatoes to the bottom of your Slow Cooker.
2. Lay the chicken on top.
3. Take a small bowl and mix in lime juice, orange juice, oil, garlic, salt, oregano, cumin and pour sauce on top of the chicken.
4. Sprinkle the sliced lemon and jalapeno on top.
5. Place the lid and cook on LOW for 6 hours.
6. Serve and enjoy!

Nutrition Values (Per Serving):

Calories: 431, Fat: 16g, Carbohydrates: 25g, Protein: 47g

Meal Prep Tip/Storage Advice: Once the dish is ready, let it cool and divide among 4 individual air tight containers. You can store them in fridge for 3 days and in the freezer for 3 months. When storing in the freezer, try to opt for containers that are specially designed for freezing at low temperatures to avoid freezer burn. Stainless steel containers are a good option. Re-heat the meal in your microwave for 3 minutes before serving.

Traditional Chicken Chili

Serving: 4 / Prep Time: 10 minutes / Cook Time: 7 hours

Ingredients:

- 7 ounces jarred salsa
- 4 chicken thighs
- 1 small yellow onion, chopped
- 7 ounces canned tomatoes, chopped
- 1 red bell pepper, chopped
- 1 tablespoon chili powder

Directions:

7. Add the salsa to your Slow cooker along with the chicken, onion, bell pepper, tomato and chili powder. Stir well and place the lid.
8. Cook on LOW for 7 hours.
9. Once ready, open the lid, serve and enjoy!

Nutrition Values (Per Serving):

Calories: 240, Fat: 3g, Carbohydrates: 17g, Protein: 8g

Meal Prep Tip/Storage Advice: Once the dish is ready, let it cool and divide among 4 individual air tight containers. You can store them in fridge for 3 days and in the freezer for 3 months. When storing in the freezer, try to opt for containers that are specially designed for freezing at low temperatures to avoid freezer burn. Stainless steel containers are a good option. Re-heat the meal in your microwave for 3 minutes before serving.

Heart Crunching Chicken Lettuce Wraps

Serving: 4 / Prep Time: 10 minutes / Cook Time: 6 hours

Ingredients:

- 2 pounds ground chicken
- 1 tablespoons honey
- ¼ cup ketchup
- ¼ cup low sodium soy sauce
- 4 cloves garlic, minced
- 2 large carrots, grated
- 1 medium sized red bell pepper, diced
- Iceberg lettuce for serving

Directions:

1. Add the above listed ingredients to your Slow Cooker. Stir well and close the lid.
2. Cook on LOW for 6 hours.Once ready, open the lid and stir well.
3. Spoon big portions of the meat on Ice Berg Lettuce leaves and serve.

Nutrition Values (Per Serving):

Calories: 313, Fat: 18g, Carbohydrates: 10g, Protein: 28g

Meal Prep Tip/Storage Advice: Once the dish is ready, let it cool and divide among 4 individual air tight containers. You can store them in fridge for 3 days and in the freezer for 3 months. When storing in the freezer, try to opt for containers that are specially designed for freezing at low temperatures to avoid freezer burn. Stainless steel containers are a good option. Re-heat the meal in your microwave for 3 minutes before serving. Make sure to use fresh lettuce when preparing the lettuce bed.

All Time Favorite Orange Chicken

Serving: 4 / Prep Time: 10 minutes / Cook Time: 6 hours

Ingredients:

- 2 pounds boneless and skinless chicken thighs
- 1 tablespoon salt
- 6 ounces orange juice concentrate
- 3 tablespoons honey
- ½ ounces, applesauce
- 1 teaspoon balsamic vinegar
- 3 tablespoons ketchup

Directions:

1. Take a bowl and add in the ketchup, balsamic vinegar, honey, applesauce, orange juice concentrate and salt. Mix well.
2. Add the chicken thighs to your Slow Cooker and pour the sauce mixture on top.
3. Close the lid and cook on LOW for 6 hours.
4. Once ready, open lid and serve hot.

Nutrition Values (Per Serving):

Calories: 309, Fat: 9g, Carbohydrates: 12g, Protein: 40g

Meal Prep Tip/Storage Advice: Once the dish is ready, let it cool and divide among 4 individual air tight containers. You can store them in fridge for 3 days and in the freezer for 3 months. When storing in the freezer, try to opt for containers that are specially designed for freezing at low temperatures to avoid freezer burn. Stainless steel containers are a good option. Re-heat the meal in your microwave for 3 minutes before serving.

Honey Pork Roast

Serving: 2 / Prep Time: 10 minutes / Cook Time: 6 hours

Ingredients:

- 1 pound pork loin roast, boneless
- 2 tablespoons honey
- ½ cup parmesan, grated
- 1 tablespoon soy sauce
- ½ tablespoon basil, dried
- ½ tablespoons oregano, dried
- 1 tablespoon garlic, minced
- 1 tablespoon olive oil
- Salt and pepper to taste
- 1 tablespoon cornstarch
- 2 tablespoons chicken stock

Directions:

1. Add the pork loin roast, honey, parmesan, soy sauce, basil, oregano, garlic, oil, pepper ad salt to your Slow Cooker. Toss well to cover the roast.
2. Place the lid and cook on LOW for 6 hours.
3. Take a small pot and mix cornstarch with stock; stir well.
4. Bring the mixture to a simmer over medium heat.
5. Transfer the roast to a cutting board and shred.
6. Add the stock mixture to your Slow cooker and give it a good stir.
7. Pour the sauce in the Slow Cooker over the shredded pork roast and serve.

Nutrition Values (Per Serving):

Calories: 374, Fat: 6g, Carbohydrates: 29g, Protein: 6g

Meal Prep Tip/Storage Advice: Once the meal is cooked, let it cool and divide among 4 individual air tight containers. Store the meal in fridge for 6 days and in your freezer for 6 months. If you want to avoid freezer burn, try storing them in the freezer proof containers such as stainless steels container. Re-heat in microwave for 5 minutes before serving.

Rosemary Pork Roast

Serving: 4 / Prep Time: 10 minutes / Cook Time: 8 hours

Ingredients:

- 3 pounds pork shoulder roast
- 1 cup bone broth
- 6 sprigs fresh rosemary
- 4 sprigs basil leaves
- 1 tablespoon chives, chopped
- ¼ teaspoon ground black pepper
- 3 organic pink lady apples, chopped

Directions:

1. Add all of the above listed ingredients.
2. Cook on LOW for about 8-10 hours.
3. Slice the roast into smaller pieces and serve!

Nutrition Values (Per Serving):

Calories: 248, Fat: 8g, Carbohydrates: 0.7g, Protein: 39g

Meal Prep Tip/Storage Advice: Once the meal is cooked, let it cool and divide among 4 individual air tight containers. Store the meal in fridge for 6 days and in your freezer for 6 months. If you want to avoid freezer burn, try storing them in the freezer proof containers such as stainless steels container. Re-heat in microwave for 5 minutes before serving.

SNACKS, BROTH AND SAUCES

Mouthwatering Sweet and Spicy Kale

Serving: 4 / Prep Time: 10 minutes / Cook Time: 8 hours

Ingredients:

- ¼ cup pure maple syrup
- 1 teaspoon garlic powder
- Juice of 1 orange
- 1 teaspoon sea salt
- ¼ teaspoon red pepper flakes
- ¼ teaspoon freshly ground black pepper
- 2 pounds of kale, stems trimmed

Directions:

1. Take a small bowl and whisk in maple syrup, garlic powder, zest, salt, orange juice, red pepper flakes and pepper.
2. Add the kale to your Slow Cooker.
3. Pour over the maple syrup mixture and toss to coat.
4. Close the lid and cook on LOW for 8 hours.
5. Once ready, open the lid and serve!

Nutrition Values (Per Serving):

Calories: 125, Fat: 11g, Carbohydrates: 29g, Protein: 5g

Meal Prep Tip/Storage Advice: Once the meal is cooked, let it cool and divide among four individual air tight containers. Store the meal in fridge for 3 days and in your freezer for 3 months. If you want to avoid freezer burn, try storing them in the freezer proof containers such as stainless steels container. Re-heat in microwave for 5 minutes before serving.

Heart Throb Caramelized Onion

Serving: 4 / Prep Time: 10 minutes / Cook Time: 8 hours

Ingredients:

- 6 onions, sliced
- 2 tablespoons oil
- ½ teaspoon salt

Directions:

1. Add the onions, oil and salt to your Slow Cooker.
2. Close the lid and cook on LOW for 8 hours.
3. Once ready, open lid and let it simmer for 2 hours until any excess water has evaporated.
4. Serve and enjoy!

Nutrition Values (Per Serving):

Calories: 126, Fat: 15g, Carbohydrates: 15g, Protein: 2g

Meal Prep Tip/Storage Advice: Once the meal is cooked, let it cool and divide among 4 individual air tight containers. Store the meal in fridge for 3 days and in your freezer for 3 months. If you want to avoid freezer burn, try storing them in the freezer proof containers such as stainless steels container. Re-heat in microwave for 5 minutes before serving.

General Purpose Mushroom Stock

Serving: 10 cups / Prep Time: 5 minutes / Cook Time: 8-10 hours

Ingredients:

- 1 onion, unpeeled, quartered from pole to pole
- 2 carrots, unpeeled, quartered
- 2 celery stalks, quartered
- 1 garlic head, unpeeled, halved across middle
- 8 ounces fresh cremini mushrooms
- 2 ounces dried porcini mushrooms
- 1 teaspoon dried thyme
- 10 peppercorns
- ½ teaspoon salt
- Enough water to fill Slow Cooker up to three quarters

Directions:

1. Add the onion, celery, carrots, garlic, mushrooms, thyme, peppercorn and water to your Slow Cooker.
2. Close the lid and cook on LOW for 8-10 hours.
3. When ready, strain the liquid through a cloth or metal mesh.
4. Discard solids and use as needed.

Nutrition Values (Per Serving):

Calories: 38, Fat: 5g, Carbohydrates: 1g, Protein: 5g

Meal Prep Tip/Storage Advice: Once the stock is cooked, let it cool and divide amongst 4 individual air tight mason jars. Store the stock in the fridge for 8-10 days and in your freezer for 3 months. If you want to avoid freezer burn, try storing them in the freezer proof containers such as stainless steels container. Re-heat in microwave for 5 minutes before serving.

Sweet and Sour Cabbage And Apples

Serving: 4 / Prep Time: 15 minutes / Cook Time: 8 hours

Ingredients:

- ¼ cup honey
- ¼ cup apple cider vinegar
- 2 tablespoons Orange Chili-Garlic Sauce
- 1 teaspoon sea salt
- 3 sweet tart apples, peeled, cored and sliced
- 2 heads, green cabbage, cored and shredded
- 1 sweet red onion, thinly sliced

Directions:

1. Take a small bowl and whisk in honey, orange-chili garlic sauce and vinegar. Stir well.
2. Add the honey mixture along with the apples, onions and cabbage to your Slow Cooker.
3. Give it a good stir and close the lid. Cook on LOW for 8 hours.
4. Serve and enjoy!

Nutrition Values (Per Serving):

Calories: 164, Fat: 1g, Carbohydrates: 41g, Protein: 4g

Meal Prep Tip/Storage Advice: Once the meal is cooked and ready, let it cool and store in 4 individual air tight containers. The dessert can be stored in the fridge for 3 days. Re-heat it for 3 minutes in microwave before serving. Freezing is not recommended and you should eat it as soon as possible.

Garlic And Herb Mushroom Crunch

Serving: 6 / Prep Time: 10 minutes / Cook Time: 8 hours

Ingredients:

- ¼ cup vegetable stock
- 2 tablespoons extra virgin olive oil
- 1 tablespoon Dijon mustard
- 1 teaspoon dried thyme
- 1 teaspoon sea salt
- ½ teaspoon dried rosemary
- ¼ teaspoon fresh ground black pepper
- 2 pounds cremini mushrooms, cleaned
- 6 garlic cloves, minced
- ¼ cup fresh parsley, chopped

Directions:

1. Take a small bowl and whisk in the vegetable stock, mustard, olive oil, salt, thyme, pepper and rosemary.
2. Add the mushrooms, garlic and the stock mixture to your Slow Cooker.
3. Close the lid and cook on LOW for 8 hours.
4. Open the lid and stir in parsley. Serve and enjoy!

Nutrition Values (Per Serving):

Calories: 92, Fat: 5g, Carbohydrates: 8g, Protein: 4g

Meal Prep Tip/Storage Advice: Once the meal is cooked, let it cool and divide among four individual air tight containers. Store the meal in the fridge for 3 days and in your freezer for 3 months. If you want to avoid freezer burn, try storing them in the freezer proof containers such as stainless steels container. Re-heat in microwave for 5 minutes before serving.

Orange And Chili Garlic Sauce

Serving: 5 cups / Prep Time: 15 minutes / Cook Time: 8 hours

Ingredients:

- ½ cup apple cider vinegar
- 4 pounds red jalapeno peppers, stems, seeds and ribs removed, chopped
- 10 garlic cloves, chopped
- ½ cup tomato paste
- Juice and zest of 1 orange
- ½ cup honey
- 2 tablespoons soy sauce
- 2 teaspoons salt

Directions:

1. Add the vinegar, garlic, peppers, tomato paste, orange juice, honey, zest, soy sauce and salt to your Slow Cooker.
2. Give it a good stir and close the lid.
3. Cook on LOW for 8 hours.
4. Use as needed!

Nutrition Values (Per Serving):

Calories: 33, Fat: 1g, Carbohydrates: 8g, Protein: 1g

Meal Prep Tip/Storage Advice: Prepare the ingredients beforehand accordingly and store them following the tips provided in the earlier section. Can be kept in air tight containers in the fridge for up to 3 days.

Exuberant Sweet Potatoes

Serving: 4 / Prep Time: 5 minutes / Cook Time: 8 hours

Ingredients:

- 6 sweet potatoes, washed and dried

Directions:

1. Loosely ball up 8 pieces of aluminum foil in the bottom of your Slow Cooker, covering about half of the surface area.
2. Prick each potato 6-8 times using a fork. Wrap each potato with foil and seal.
3. Place the wrapped potatoes in the cooker on top of the foil bed.
4. Place the lid and cook on LOW for 8 hours. Use tongs to remove the potatoes and unwrap them.

Nutrition Values (Per Serving):

Calories: 129, Fat: 0g, Carbohydrates: 30g, Protein: 2g

Meal Prep Tip/Storage Advice: Once the meal is cooked, let it cool and divide among four individual air tight containers. Store the meal in the fridge for 3 days and in your freezer for 3 months. If you want to avoid freezer burn, try storing them in the freezer proof containers such as stainless steels container. Re-heat in microwave for 5 minutes before serving.

Wow-Spaghetti Squash

Serving: 6 / Prep Time: 5 minutes / Cook Time: 8 hours

Ingredients:

- 1 spaghetti squash
- 2 cups water

Directions:

1. Wash the squash with soap and water. Rinse it well.
2. Skewer with fork, puncture 6 holes. Place the squash in your Slow Cooker. Add the water and cover with a lid. Cook on LOW for 8 hours.

3. Once ready, transfer the squash to a cutting board and let it cool.
4. Then, cut it in half and discard the seeds.
5. Use two forks to scrape out the squash stands and transfer to a bowl.
6. Serve and enjoy!

Nutrition Values (Per Serving):

Calories: 52, Fat: 0g, Carbohydrates: 12g, Protein: 1g

Meal Prep Tip/Storage Advice: Once the meal is cooked, let it cool and divide among 6 individual air tight containers. Store the meal in the fridge for 3 days and in your freezer for 3 months. If you want to avoid freezer burn, try storing them in the freezer proof containers such as stainless steels container. Re-heat in microwave for 5 minutes before serving.

Bacon –Wrapped Drumsticks

Serving: 6 / Prep Time: 10 minutes / Cook Time: 8 hours

Ingredients:

- 12 chicken drumsticks
- 12 slices thin-cut bacon

Directions:

1. Wrap each chicken drumstick in bacon.
2. Place the drumsticks in your Slow Cooker.
3. Seal the lid and cook on LOW for 8 hours.
4. Serve and enjoy!

Nutrition Values (Per Serving):

Calories: 202, Fat: 8g, Carbohydrates: 0g, Protein: 30g

Meal Prep Tip/Storage Advice: Once the meal is cooked, let it cool and divide among 6 individual air tight containers. Store the meal in the fridge for 3 days and in your freezer for 3 months.

All-Purpose Bone Broth

Serving: 10 cups / Prep Time: 5 minutes / Cook Time: 12/ 24 hours

Ingredients:

- 3 pounds poultry, pork, lamb or beef bones
- 1 garlic head, unpeeled, halved across middle
- 1 onion, unpeeled, quartered pole to pole
- 2 carrots, unpeeled and halved
- 2 celery stalks, unpeeled and halved
- 1 tablespoons apple cider vinegar
- 2 dried bay leaves
- 2 fresh rosemary sprigs
- 2 fresh thyme sprigs
- 10 peppercorns
- ½ teaspoon salt
- Enough water to fill ¾ of the Crock Pot

Directions:

1. Add the bones, onions, garlic, celery, carrots, vinegar, bay leaves, thyme, rosemary, peppercorns, salt and water to your Slow Cooker.
2. Close the lid and cook on LOW for 12 hours (for poultry) and 24 hours (if pork, lamb or beef bones).
3. Once ready, strain the liquid through a cloth or metal mesh.
4. Discard solids and use as needed.

Nutrition Values (Per Serving):

Calories: 38, Fat: 5g, Carbohydrates: 1g, Protein: 5g

Meal Prep Tip/Storage Advice: Prepare the ingredients beforehand accordingly and store them following the tips provided in the earlier section. Can be kept in air tight containers in the fridge for up to 1-2 weeks.

Everyday Vegetable Stock

Serving: 10 cups / Prep Time: 5 minutes / Cook Time: 8 hours

Ingredients:

- 2 celery stalks (with leaves), quartered
- 4 ounces mushrooms, with stems
- 2 carrots, unpeeled and quartered
- 1 onion, unpeeled, quartered from pole to pole
- 1 garlic head, unpeeled, halved across middle
- 2 fresh thyme sprigs
- 10 peppercorns
- ½ teaspoon salt
- Enough water to fill 3 quarters of Slow Cooker

Directions:

1. Add celery, mushrooms, onion, carrots, garlic, thyme, salt, peppercorn and water to your Slow Cooker.
2. Give it a good stir and cover with the lid.
3. Cook on LOW for 8 hours.
4. Strain the stock through a fine mesh cloth or metal mesh, and discard solids. Use as needed.

Nutrition Values (Per Serving):

Calories: 38, Fat: 5g, Carbohydrates: 1g, Protein: 0g

Meal Prep Tip/Storage Advice: Prepare the ingredients beforehand accordingly and store them following the tips provided in the earlier section. Can be kept in air tight containers in the fridge for up to 1-2 weeks.

The Vegan Lovers Refried Beans Dip

Serving: 12 / Prep Time: 5 minutes / Cook Time: 10 hours

Ingredients:

- 4 cups vegetable broth
- 4 cups water
- 3 cups dried pinto beans
- 1 onion, chopped
- 2 jalapeno peppers, minced
- 4 garlic cloves, minced
- 1 tablespoon chili powder
- 2 teaspoons ground cumin
- 1 teaspoon sweet paprika
- 1 teaspoon salt
- ½ teaspoon fresh ground black pepper

Directions:

1. Add the above listed ingredients to your Slow Cooker.
2. Cover and cook on HIGH for 10 hours.
3. If there is extra liquid, ladle the liquid up and reserve it in a bowl.
4. Use an immersion blender to blend the mixture (inside the Slow Cooker) until smooth.
5. Add the reserved liquid. Serve hot and enjoy!

Nutrition Values (Per Serving):

Calories: 91, Fat: 0g, Carbohydrates: 16g, Protein: 5g

Meal Prep Tip/Storage Advice: Once the meal is cooked, let it cool and divide among 6 individual air tight containers. Store the meal in the fridge for 3 days and in your freezer for 3 months. If you want to avoid freezer burn, try storing them in the freezer proof containers such as stainless steels container. Re-heat in microwave for 5 minutes before serving.

Satisfying Garlic Chicken Livers

Serving: 4 / Prep Time: minutes / Cook Time: 8 hours

Ingredients:

- 1 pound chicken livers
- 8 garlic cloves, minced
- 8 ounces cremini mushrooms, quartered
- 4 slices uncooked bacon, chopped
- 1 onion, chopped
- 1 cup bone broth
- 1 teaspoon dried thyme
- 1 teaspoon dried rosemary
- 1 teaspoon salt
- 1 teaspoon freshly ground black pepper
- ¼ cup fresh parsley, chopped

Directions:

1. Add the livers, garlic, bacon, mushrooms, onion, broth, thyme, rosemary to your Slow Cooker.
2. Season with salt and pepper and give it a good stir.
3. Close the lid and cook on LOW for 8 hours.
4. Open the lid and sprinkle with parsley.
5. Stir, serve and enjoy!

Nutrition Values (Per Serving):

Calories: 210, Fat: 9g, Carbohydrates: 6g, Protein: 24g

Meal Prep Tip/Storage Advice: Once the meal is cooked, let it cool and divide among 4 individual air tight containers. Store the meal in the fridge for 3 days and in your freezer for 3 months. If you want to avoid freezer burn, try storing them in the freezer proof containers such as stainless steels container. Re-heat in microwave for 5 minutes before serving.

Honey Glaze Chicken Wings

Serving: 4 / Prep Time: 10 minutes / Cook Time: 8 hours

Ingredients:

- ¼ cup honey
- Juice of 1 lime
- Zest of 1 lime
- 3 jalapeno peppers, minced
- 2 tablespoons soy sauce
- 1 teaspoon garlic powder
- ¼ teaspoon fresh ground black pepper
- 3 pounds chicken wings, separated into drummettes and wings

Directions:

1. Take a small bowl and whisk in honey, zest, lime juice, jalapenos, soy sauce, garlic powder and pepper.
2. Stir and transfer the mixture to the Slow Cooker.
3. Add in the chicken wings and toss to coat them well.
4. Close the lid and cook on LOW for 8 hours.
5. Serve and enjoy!

Nutrition Values (Per Serving):

Calories: 365, Fat: 13g, Carbohydrates: 11g, Protein: 49g

Meal Prep Tip/Storage Advice: Once the meal is cooked, let it cool and divide among 4 individual air tight containers. Store the meal in the fridge for 3 days and in your freezer for 3 months. If you want to avoid freezer burn, try storing them in the freezer proof containers such as stainless steels container. Re-heat in microwave for 5 minutes before serving.

FISH & SEAFOOD

Spicy Tuna Dish

Serving: 3 / Prep Time: 10 minutes / Cook Time: 4 hours 10 minutes

Ingredients:

- ½ pound tuna loin, cubed
- 1 garlic clove, minced
- 4 jalapeno peppers, chopped
- 1 cup olive oil, some of it for greasing
- 3 red chili peppers, chopped
- 2 teaspoons black peppercorns, ground
- 1 pinch of salt
- Black pepper to taste

Directions:

1. Grease your Slow Cooker with oil.
2. Add chili peppers, jalapeno, salt, pepper, peppercorns, garlic and whisk well in your Crock Pot Slow Cooker.
3. Place the lid and cook on LOW for 4 hours.
4. Then, carefully open the lid and add tuna.
5. Toss and place the lid back on. Cook on HIGH for 10 more minutes.
6. Once ready, serve and enjoy immediately.

Nutrition Values (Per Serving):

Calories: 200, Fat: 4g, Carbohydrates: 16g, Protein: 4g

Meal Prep Tip/Storage Advice: Once the meal is cooked, let it cool and divide among three individual air tight containers. Store the meal in the fridge for 3 days and in your freezer for 3 months. If you want to avoid freezer burn, try storing them in the freezer proof containers such as stainless steels container. Re-heat in microwave for 5 minutes before serving.

Lemon Halibut And Capers

Serving: 4 / Prep Time: 10 minutes / Cook Time: 8 hours

Ingredients:

- Juice of 2 lemons
- ¼ cup capers, drained
- Zest of 1 lemon
- 6 cups fish stock
- 3 carrots, peeled and chopped
- 2 red bell peppers, seeds and ribs removed, chopped
- 2 zucchini, chopped
- ½ teaspoon garlic powder
- ½ teaspoon sea salt
- ¼ teaspoon fresh ground black pepper
- 1 ½ pounds halibut steak, skin and bones removed, cut into 1 inch cubes
- ¼ cup fresh parsley, chopped

Directions:

1. Add the lemon juice, zest, capers, fish stock, carrots, zucchini, bell pepper, garlic powder, pepper and salt to your Slow Cooker.
2. Stir and close the lid. Cook on LOW for 7 ½ hours.
3. Once ready, open the lid and add the halibut.
4. Place the lid back and cook on HIGH for 30 minutes until the halibut is cooked thoroughly.
5. Carefully open the lid and stir in parsley. Serve and enjoy!

Nutrition Values (Per Serving):

Calories: 190, Fat: 3g, Carbohydrates: 8g, Protein: 32g

Meal Prep Tip/Storage Advice: Once the meal is cooked, let it cool and divide among four individual air tight containers. Store the meal in the fridge for 3 days and in your freezer for 3 months.

Asparagus and Tilapia Platter

Serving: 4 / Prep Time: 20 minutes / Cook Time: 2 hours

Ingredients:

- A bunch of asparagus
- 6 Tilapia fillets
- 8-12 tablespoons lemon juice
- Pepper for seasoning
- Lemon juice for seasoning
- ½ tablespoons coconut oil (for each fillet)

Directions:

1. Cut single pieces of foil for the fillets.
2. Divide the bundle of asparagus into even number depending on the number of your fillets.
3. Lay the fillets on each of the pieces of foil.
4. Sprinkle pepper and add a teaspoon of lemon juice.
5. Add clarified butter and top with asparagus.
6. Fold the foil over the fish and seal the ends.
7. Repeat with all the fillets and transfer to the Crock Pot Slow Cooker.
8. Cover the lid and cook on HIGH for 2 hours.
9. Once ready, open the lid and serve immediately.

Nutrition Values (Per Serving):

Calories: 229, Fat: 10g, Carbohydrates: 1g, Protein: 28g

Meal Prep Tip/Storage Advice: Once the meal is cooked, let it cool and divide among four individual air tight containers. Store the meal in the fridge for 3 days and in your freezer for 3 months. If you want to avoid freezer burn, try storing them in the freezer proof containers such as stainless steels container. Re-heat in microwave for 5 minutes before serving.

Climactic Seafood Chowder

Serving: 3 / Prep Time: 10 minutes / Cook Time: 8 hours 30 minutes

Ingredients:

- 1 cup water
- ½ fennel bulb, chopped
- 1 sweet potato, cubed
- ½ yellow onion, chopped
- 1 bay leaf
- ½ tablespoon thyme, dried
- ½ celery rib, chopped
- Salt and pepper to taste
- 1 pinch cayenne pepper
- ½ bottle clam juice
- 1 tablespoon white flour
- ½ cup milk
- ½ pounds salmon fillets, cubed
- 1 sea scallops, halved
- 12 shrimp, peeled and deveined
- 2 tablespoons parsley, chopped

Directions:

1. Pour the water, and add fennel, onion, potatoes, bay leaves, thyme, celery, clam juice, cayenne, salt, pepper to your Crock Pot Slow Cooker.
2. Stir well and cover with the lid. Cook on LOW for 8 hours.
3. Once ready, open the lid and salmon, milk, flour, scallops, shrimp and parsley. Stir and place the lid, cook on LOW for 30 minutes more.

Nutrition Values (Per Serving):

Calories: 293, Fat: 24g, Carbohydrates: 4g, Protein: 16g

Meal Prep Tip/Storage Advice: Once the dish is ready, let it cool and divide the dish amongst 3 individual air tight zip bags. You can store them in the fridge for 3 days and in the freezer for 3 months. When storing in the freezer, try to opt for containers that are specially designed for freezing at low temperatures to avoid freezer burn. Stainless steel containers are a good option. Re-heat the meal in your microwave for 3 minutes before serving.

Coconut Clam Bites

Serving: 3 / Prep Time: 10 minutes / Cook Time: 6 hours

Ingredients:

- 10 ounces canned clams, chopped
- ¼ cup coconut milk
- 2 eggs, whisked
- 1 tablespoon olive oil
- 1 green bell pepper, chopped
- 1 yellow onion, chopped
- Pinch of salt and black pepper (each)

Directions:

1. Add the clams to your Crock Pot Slow Cooker.
2. Stir in milk, eggs, oil, bell pepper, onion.
3. Season with salt and pepper and give it a good stir.
4. Place the lid and cook on LOW for 6 hours.
5. Once ready, open the lid and divide among individual serving bowls.

Nutrition Values (Per Serving):

Calories: 270, Fat: 4g, Carbohydrates: 13g, Protein: 7g

Meal Prep Tip/Storage Advice: Once the meal is cooked, let it cool and divide among three individual air tight containers. Store the meal in the fridge for 3 days and in your freezer for 3 months.

Juicy Asian Salmon Fillets

Serving: 3 / Prep Time: 10 minutes / Cook Time: 3 hours

Ingredients:

- 2 medium salmon fillets
- Salt and pepper to taste
- 2 tablespoons soy sauce
- 2 tablespoons maple syrup
- 16 ounces broccoli
- 2 tablespoons lemon juice
- 1 teaspoon sesame seeds

Directions:

1. Add the broccoli florets in your Crock Pot Slow Cooker.
2. Top with fillets.
3. Take a bowl and mix in maple syrup, soy sauce, lemon juice.
4. Whisk well and pour over the salmon.
5. Season with salt and pepper.
6. Place the lid and cook on LOW for 3 hours.
7. Once ready, open the lid and serve hot.

Nutrition Values (Per Serving):

Calories: 230, Fat: 4g, Carbohydrates: 7g, Protein: 6g

Meal Prep Tip/Storage Advice: Once the meal is cooked, let it cool and divide among three individual air tight containers. Store the meal in the fridge for 3 days and in your freezer for 3 months. If you want to avoid freezer burn, try storing them in the freezer proof containers such as stainless steels container. Re-heat in microwave for 5 minutes before serving.

Delicious Shrimp Scampi

Serving: 3 / Prep Time: 20 minutes / Cook Time: 2 hours and 30 minutes

Ingredients:

- ¼ cup chicken broth
- ½ cup white wine vinegar
- 2 tablespoons olive oil
- 2 teaspoons garlic, chopped
- 2 teaspoons parsley, minced
- 1 pound large raw shrimp, peeled and deveined

Directions:

1. Add the chicken broth, lemon juice, white wine vinegar, olive oil, lemon juice, chopped garlic and fresh minced parsley.
2. Then, add in the thawed shrimp. The ratio should be 1 pound of shrimp for ¼ cup of chicken broth.
3. Place the lid and cook on LOW for 2 ½ hours.
4. Once ready, open the lid and serve immediately.

Nutrition Values (Per Serving):

Calories: 293, Fat: 24g, Carbohydrates: 4g, Protein: 16g

Meal Prep Tip/Storage Advice: Once the meal is cooked, let it cool and divide among three individual air tight containers. Store the meal in the fridge for 3 days and in your freezer for 3 months. If you want to avoid freezer burn, try storing them in the freezer proof containers such as stainless steels container. Re-heat in microwave for 5 minutes before serving.

Ultimately Simple Slow Cook Salmon

Serving: 3 / Prep Time: 10 minutes / Cook Time: 2 hours

Ingredients:

- 2 medium salmon fillets, boneless
- 1 pinch of nutmeg
- 1 pinch of cloves
- 1 pinch of ginger
- 1 pinch salt and pepper, each
- 2 teaspoons sugar
- 1 teaspoon onion powder
- ¼ teaspoon chipotle chili powder
- ½ teaspoon cayenne pepper
- ½ teaspoon cinnamon, ground

Directions:

1. Take a bowl and add the salmon fillets, cloves, nutmeg, ginger, salt, coconut sugar, onion powder, chili powder, cayenne pepper, cinnamon and toss.
2. Divide the mixture between 2 tin foil pieces.
3. Wrap them and place in your Crock Pot Slow Cooker.
4. Place the lid and cook on LOW for 2 hours.
5. Once ready, open the lid and serve immediately.

Nutrition Values (Per Serving):

Calories: 220, Fat: 13g, Carbohydrates: 16g, Protein: 4g

Meal Prep Tip/Storage Advice: Once the meal is cooked, let it cool and divide among three individual air tight containers. Store the meal in the fridge for 3 days and in your freezer for 3 months. If you want to avoid freezer burn, try storing them in the freezer proof containers such as stainless steels container. Re-heat in microwave for 5 minutes before serving.

VEGETARIAN AND VEGETABLES

Sweet Potato And Leek Soup

Serving: 6 / Prep Time: 10 minutes / Cook Time: 8 hours

Ingredients:

- 6 cups sweet potatoes, peeled and cubed
- 2 leeks, whites and greens, sliced
- 6 cups vegetable stock
- 1 teaspoon dried thyme
- 1 teaspoon salt
- ¼ teaspoon fresh ground black pepper

Directions:

1. Add the sweet potatoes, leeks, thyme, stock, salt and pepper to your Crock Pot Slow Cooker. Close the lid and cook on LOW for 8 hours.
2. Mash with potato masher and use an immersion blender to smoothen the soup.
3. Serve and enjoy!

Nutrition Values (Per Serving):

Calories: 234, Fat: 2g, Carbohydrates: 47g, Protein: 8g

Meal Prep Tip/Storage Advice: Once the dish is ready, let it cool and divide the dish amongst 6 individual air tight zip bags. You can store them in the fridge for 3 days and in the freezer for 3 months. When storing in the freezer, try to opt for containers that are specially designed for freezing at low temperatures to avoid freezer burn. Stainless steel containers/thick glass mason jars/freezer zip bags are a good option. Re-heat the meal in your microwave for 3 minutes before serving.

Lemon And Artichoke Dish

Serving: 4 / Prep Time: 10 minutes / Cook Time: 5 hours

Ingredients:

- 5 large artichokes
- 1 teaspoon sea salt
- 2 celery stalks, sliced
- 2 large carrots, cut into matchsticks
- ¼ teaspoon black pepper
- 1 teaspoon dried thyme
- 1 tablespoon dried rosemary
- Lemon wedge for garnish

Directions:

1. Remove the stalk from the artichokes and remove the tough outer shell.
2. Transfer the chokes to your Crock Pot Slow Cooker and add 2 cups of boiling water.
3. Add celery, lemon juice, salt, carrots, black pepper, thyme, rosemary.
4. Cook on HIGH for 4 hours.
5. Serve the artichokes with lemon wedges.

Nutrition Values (Per Serving):

Calories: 205, Fat: 2g, Carbohydrates: 12g, Protein: 34g

Meal Prep Tip/Storage Advice: Once the meal is cooked, let it cool and divide among 4 individual air tight containers. Store the meal in the fridge for 3 days and in your freezer for 3 months. If you want to avoid freezer burn, try storing them in the freezer proof containers such as stainless steels container. Re-heat in microwave for 5 minutes before serving.

Maple And Thyme Brussels

Serving: 2 / Prep Time: 10 minutes / Cook Time: 3 hours

Ingredients:

- 1 small red onion, chopped
- ½ pound Brussels sprouts, trimmed and halved
- 1 pinch of salt and pepper
- 2 tablespoons apple juice
- 1 tablespoon olive oil
- 2 tablespoons maple syrup
- 1 tablespoon thyme, chopped

Directions:

1. Add sprouts, onions, salt, pepper, apple juice to your Crock Pot Slow Cooker.
2. Toss well to coat everything.
3. Place the lid and cook on LOW for 3 hours.
4. Take another bowl and add maple syrup, oil and thyme.
5. Whisk well and pour the mixture over sprouts, once they are cooked.
6. Divide between platters and serve.

Nutrition Values (Per Serving):

Calories: 170, Fat: 4g, Carbohydrates: 14g, Protein: 6g

Meal Prep Tip/Storage Advice: Once the meal is cooked, let it cool and divide among 2 individual air tight containers. Store the meal in the fridge for 3 days and in your freezer for 3 months. If you want to avoid freezer burn, try storing them in the freezer proof containers such as stainless steels container. Re-heat in microwave for 5 minutes before serving.

Rapid Broccoli Crunches

Serving: 4 / Prep Time: 10 minutes / Cook Time: 3 hours

Ingredients:

- 2 cups broccoli florets
- 2 ounces cream of celery soup
- 2 tablespoons cheddar cheese, shredded
- 1 small yellow onion, chopped
- ¼ teaspoon Worcestershire sauce
- Salt and pepper to taste
- 10 butter flavored crackers, crushed
- ½ tablespoon butter

Directions:

1. Add the broccoli, cream, cheese, cheddar, onion, sauce, crackers to your Crock Pot Slow Cooker.
2. Season with salt and pepper, and toss well.
3. Place the lid and cook on LOW for 3 hours.
4. Once ready, open the lid and serve immediately.

Nutrition Values (Per Serving):

Calories: 162, Fat: 11g, Carbohydrates: 11g, Protein: 5g

Meal Prep Tip/Storage Advice: Once the meal is cooked, let it cool and divide among 4 individual air tight containers. Store the meal in the fridge for 3 days and in your freezer for 3 months. If you want to avoid freezer burn, try storing them in the freezer proof containers such as stainless steels container. Re-heat in microwave for 5 minutes before serving.

Hand-In-Hand Potato Hash

Serving: 2 / Prep Time: 10 minutes / Cook Time: 4 hours

Ingredients:

- 1 medium orange pepper, diced
- 1 medium yellow pepper, diced
- 3 ½ ounces butternut squash, diced
- 10 ½ ounces sweet potatoes, diced
- 2 medium tomatoes, thinly diced
- 1 tablespoon coconut oil
- 1 teaspoon garlic puree
- 1 teaspoon Mustard powder
- Salt and pepper to taste

Directions:

1. Dice all the vegetables and potatoes. Transfer them to your Slow Cooker.
2. Add the coconut oil and seasoning. Mix well.
3. Cover with the lid and cook on LOW for 4 hours.
4. Once ready, open the lid and serve immediately.

Nutrition Values (Per Serving):

Calories: 270, Fat: 10g, Carbohydrates: 39g, Protein: 5g

Meal Prep Tip/Storage Advice: Once the meal is cooked, let it cool and divide among 2 individual air tight containers. Store the meal in the fridge for 3 days and in your freezer for 3 months. If you want to avoid freezer burn, try storing them in the freezer proof containers such as stainless steels container. Re-heat in microwave for 5 minutes before serving.

Pumpkin Curry Soup

Serving: 6 / Prep Time: 10 minutes / Cook Time: 8 hours

Ingredients:

- 2 cans (29 ounces) pumpkin puree
- 1 onion, chopped
- 5 cups vegetable stock
- 1 teaspoon garlic powder
- 1 teaspoon garam masala
- 1 teaspoon curry powder
- 1 teaspoon salt
- ½ teaspoon ground ginger
- 2 tablespoons fresh cilantro, chopped
- 1 cup coconut milk

Directions:

1. In your Crock Pot Slow Cooker, stir in the pumpkin, stock, garlic powder, curry powder, garam masala, salt and ginger.
2. Close the lid and cook on LOW for 8 hours.
3. Once ready, open the lid and stir in cilantro, coconut milk.
4. Serve and enjoy!

Nutrition Values (Per Serving):

Calories: 228, Fat: 12g, Carbohydrates: 28g, Protein: 8g

Meal Prep Tip/Storage Advice: Once the dish is ready, let it cool and divide the dish amongst 6 individual air tight zip bags. You can store them in the fridge for 3 days and in the freezer for 3 months. When storing in the freezer, try to opt for containers that are specially designed for freezing at low temperatures to avoid freezer burn. Stainless steel containers/ thick glass mason jars/ freezer zip bags are good options. Re-heat the meal in your microwave for 3 minutes before serving.

Acorn Squash With Mango Chutney

Serving: 4 / Prep Time: 10 minutes / Cook Time: 3 hours 10 minutes

Ingredients:

- 1 large acorn squash
- ¼ cup mango chutney
- ¼ cup flaked coconut
- Salt and pepper to taste

Directions:

1. Cut the squash in quarters, remove the seeds, and discard the stingy pulp.
2. Spray your Crock Pot Slow Cooker with olive oil.
3. Transfer the squash to the cooker.
4. Take a bowl and mix in the coconut and chutney. Transfer the mixture into the center of the squash and season well.
5. Place the lid on and cook on LOW for 2.5-3 hours.
6. Once ready, open the lid and serve immediately.

Nutrition Values (Per Serving):

Calories: 226, Fat: 6g, Carbohydrates: 24g, Protein: 17g

Meal Prep Tip/Storage Advice: Once the meal is cooked, let it cool and divide among 4 individual air tight containers. Store the meal in the fridge for 3 days and in your freezer for 3 months. If you want to avoid freezer burn, try storing them in the freezer proof containers such as stainless steels container. Re-heat in microwave for 5 minutes before serving.

Pure Maple Glazed Carrots

Serving: 6 / Prep Time: 10 minutes / Cook Time: 8 hours

Ingredients:

- ¼ cup pure maple syrup
- ½ teaspoon ground ginger
- ¼ teaspoon ground nutmeg
- ½ teaspoon salt
- Juice of 1 orange
- 1 pound baby carrots

Directions:

1. Take a small bowl and whisk in THE syrup, nutmeg, ginger, salt, orange juice.
2. Add the carrots to your Crock Pot Slow Cooker and pour the syrup over.
3. Toss to coat, close the lid and cook on LOW for 8 hours.
4. Once ready, open the lid and serve immediately.

Nutrition Values (Per Serving):

Calories: 76, Fat: 1g, Carbohydrates: 19g, Protein: 76g

Meal Prep Tip/Storage Advice: Once the meal is cooked, let it cool and divide among 6 individual air tight containers. Store the meal in the fridge for 3 days and in your freezer for 3 months. If you want to avoid freezer burn, try storing them in the freezer proof containers such as stainless steels container. Re-heat in microwave for 5 minutes before serving.

Curiously Slow Cooker Brussels

Serving: 4 / Prep Time: 15 minutes / Cook Time: 4 hours

Ingredients:

- 1 pound Brussels sprouts, bottom trimmed and cut
- 1 tablespoon olive oil
- 1 tablespoons Dijon mustard
- ¼ cup water
- Salt and pepper to taste
- ½ teaspoon dried tarragon

Directions:

1. Place the Brussels, mustard, water, salt and pepper to your Slow Cooker.
2. Add dried tarragon and stir well.
3. Cover with the lid and cook on LOW for 5 hours, or until the Brussels are very tender.
4. Once ready, open the lid and add Dijon over the Brussels.
5. Serve and enjoy!

Nutrition Values (Per Serving):

Calories: 83, Fat: 4g, Carbohydrates: 11g, Protein: 4g

Meal Prep Tip/Storage Advice: Once the meal is cooked, let it cool and divide among 4 individual air tight containers. Store the meal in the fridge for 3 days and in your freezer for 3 months. If you want to avoid freezer burn, try storing them in the freezer proof containers such as stainless steels container. Re-heat in microwave for 5 minutes before serving.

Ginger and Orange "Beets"

Serving: 6 / Prep Time: 20 minutes / Cook Time: 8 hours

Ingredients:

- 2 pounds beets, peeled and cut into wedges
- Juice of 2 oranges
- Zest of 1 orange
- 1 teaspoon fresh ginger, grated
- 1 tablespoon honey
- 1 tablespoon apple cider vinegar
- ⅛ teaspoon fresh ground black pepper
- Sea salt to taste

Directions:

1. Add the beets, zest, orange juice, ginger, honey, pepper, salt and vinegar to your Crock Pot Slow Cooker.
2. Stir well, close the lid and cook on LOW for 8 hours.
3. Once ready, open the lid and serve immediately.

Nutrition Values (Per Serving):

Calories: 108, Fat: 1g, Carbohydrates: 25g, Protein: 3g

Meal Prep Tip/Storage Advice: Once the meal is cooked, let it cool and divide among 6 individual air tight containers. Store the meal in the fridge for 3 days and in your freezer for 3 months. If you want to avoid freezer burn, try storing them in the freezer proof containers such as stainless steels container. Re-heat in microwave for 5 minutes before serving.

Mysterious Pineapple Rice

Serving: 2 / Prep Time: 10 minutes / Cook Time: 2 hours

Ingredients:

- 1 cup rice
- 2 cups water
- 1 small cauliflower, florets separated and chopped
- ½ small pineapple, peeled and chopped
- Salt and pepper to taste
- 1 teaspoon olive oil

Directions:

1. Add the rice, cauliflower, pineapple, water, oil, salt and pepper to your Crock Pot Slow Cooker. Stir gently.
2. Place the lid and cook on HIGH for 2 hours.
3. Once ready, open the lid and fluff the rice with a fork.
4. Season with salt and pepper if needed.
5. Divide between serving platters and enjoy!

Nutrition Values (Per Serving):

Calories: 152, Fat: 4g, Carbohydrates: 18g, Protein: 4g

Meal Prep Tip/Storage Advice: Once the meal is cooked, let it cool and divide among 2 individual air tight containers. Store the meal in the fridge for 3 days and in your freezer for 3 months. If you want to avoid freezer burn, try storing them in the freezer proof containers such as stainless steels container. Re-heat in microwave for 5 minutes before serving.

Out Of This World Sweet Brussels

Serving: 6 / Prep Time: 10 minutes / Cook Time: 8 hours

Ingredients:

- Juice and zest of 1 orange
- 2 tablespoons Orange-Chili-Garlic Sauce
- ¼ cup pure maple syrup
- ¼ cup apple cider vinegar
- 1 teaspoon garlic powder
- 1 teaspoon salt
- 1 pound Brussels sprouts, halved pole to pole

Directions:

1. Take a small bowl and whisk in orange juice, orange chili garlic sauce, zest, maple syrup, vinegar, garlic powder and salt. Stir well.
2. Add the Brussels to your Crock Pot Slow Cooker.
3. Pour the sauce mixture on top and give it a good stir.
4. Close the lid and cook on LOW for 8 hours.
5. Once ready, open the lid and serve hot.

Nutrition Values (Per Serving):

Calories: 99, Fat: 16g, Carbohydrates: 24g, Protein: 3g

Meal Prep Tip/Storage Advice: Once the meal is cooked, let it cool and divide among 6 individual air tight containers. Store the meal in the fridge for 3 days and in your freezer for 3 months. If you want to avoid freezer burn, try storing them in the freezer proof containers such as stainless steels container. Re-heat in microwave for 5 minutes before serving.

Jackfruit And Chickpeas Cocktail

Serving: 4 / Prep Time: 10 minutes / Cook Time: 6-8 hours

Ingredients:

- 1 can (20 ounce) young jackfruit, in water, drained
- 1 can (15 ounce) chickpeas, rinsed and drained
- 1 can (15 ounce) diced tomatoes, with juice
- 1 can (15 ounce) full-fat coconut milk
- 1 cup low sodium vegetable broth
- 1 onion, diced
- 3 garlic cloves, minced
- A handful of fresh cilantro leaves
- 2 teaspoons curry powder
- 1 ½ teaspoons ground ginger
- 1 teaspoon ground coriander
- ½ teaspoon ground turmeric
- ½ teaspoon salt

Directions:

1. Add the above listed ingredients to your Crock Pot Slow Cooker.
2. Give it a good stir and place the lid.
3. Cook on LOW for 6-8 hours.
4. Once ready, open the lid and serve immediately.

Nutrition Values (Per Serving):

Calories: 536, Fat: 37g, Carbohydrates: 38g, Protein: 18g

Meal Prep Tip/Storage Advice: Once the meal is cooked, let it cool and divide among 4 individual air tight containers. Store the meal in the fridge for 3 days and in your freezer for 3 months. Fruits are not good for freezing so it's better not to freeze this dish. Re-heat in microwave for 5 minutes before serving.

Cream Dredged Corn Platter

Serving: 3 / Prep Time: 10 minutes / Cook Time: 4 hours

Ingredients:

- 3 cups corn
- 2 ounces cream cheese, cubed
- 2 tablespoons milk
- 2 tablespoons whipping cream
- 2 tablespoon butter, melted
- Salt and pepper to taste
- 2 bacon strips, cooked and crumbled
- 1 tablespoon green onion, chopped

Directions:

1. Add the corn, cream cheese, milk, whipping cream, butter, salt and pepper to your Crock Pot Slow Cooker.
2. Give it a nice toss to mix everything well.
3. Place the lid and cook on LOW for 4 hours.
4. Once ready, open the lid and divide among serving platters.
5. Scatter bacon and green onions on top.
6. Serve and enjoy!

Nutrition Values (Per Serving):

Calories: 261, Fat: 11g, Carbohydrates: 17g, Protein: 6g

Meal Prep Tip/Storage Advice: Once the meal is cooked, let it cool and divide among 4 individual air tight containers. Store the meal in the fridge for 3 days and in your freezer for 3 months. If you want to avoid freezer burn, try storing them in the freezer proof containers such as stainless steels container. Re-heat in microwave for 5 minutes before serving.

Cabbage Delight

Serving: 6 / Prep Time: 15 minutes / Cook Time: 6- 8 hours

Ingredients:

- ½ cup water
- 1 head green cabbage, cored and chopped
- 1 pound sweet potatoes, peeled and chopped
- 3 carrots, peeled and chopped
- 1 onion, sliced
- 1 teaspoon extra virgin olive oil
- ½ teaspoon ground turmeric
- ½ teaspoon ground cumin
- ¼ teaspoon ground ginger

Directions:

1. Pour water in your Crock Pot Slow Cooker.
2. Take a medium bowl and add the cabbage, carrots, potatoes, onion and mix well.
3. Add olive oil, turmeric, ginger, cumin and toss until the veggies are fully coated.
4. Transfer the veggie mixture to your Slow Cooker.
5. Cover and cook on LOW for 6-8 hours.
6. Once ready, open the lid and serve immediately.

Nutrition Values (Per Serving):

Calories: 155, Fat: 2g, Carbohydrates: 35g, Protein: 4g

Meal Prep Tip/Storage Advice: Once the meal is cooked, let it cool and divide among 4 individual air tight containers. Store the meal in the fridge for 3 days and in your freezer for 3 months. If you want to avoid freezer burn, try storing them in the freezer proof containers such as stainless steels container. Re-heat in microwave for 5 minutes before serving.

Unique Carrot Mix

Serving: 3 / Prep Time: 10 minutes / Cook Time: 8 hours

Ingredients:

- ½ pound carrots, sliced
- 1 pinch of salt and pepper
- ½ tablespoons water
- 2 tablespoons sugar
- ½ tablespoons olive oil
- ½ teaspoon orange rind, grated

Directions:

1. Pour the oil to your Crock Pot Slow Cooker. Grease well.
2. Add in the carrots, water, sugar, salt, pepper, orange rind to and toss well.
3. Place the lid and cook on LOW for 8 hours.
4. Once ready, open the lid and serve immediately.

Nutrition Values (Per Serving):

Calories: 140, Fat: 2g, Carbohydrates: 7g, Protein: 6g

Meal Prep Tip/Storage Advice: Once the meal is cooked, let it cool and divide among 4 individual air tight containers. Store the meal in the fridge for 3 days and in your freezer for 3 months. If you want to avoid freezer burn, try storing them in the freezer proof containers such as stainless steels container. Re-heat in microwave for 5 minutes before serving.

Hearty Butternut Squash Soup

Serving: 6 / Prep Time: 15 minutes / Cook Time: 6 hours

Ingredients:

- 1 whole onion, chopped
- 3 carrots, peeled and chopped
- 3 garlic cloves, minced
- 1 butternut squash, peeled, seeded and chopped
- 4 cups vegetable broth

Directions:

1. Add the above listed ingredients to the Crock Pot and cook on LOW for 6 hours, or until the squash is tender.
2. Once ready, open the lid.
3. Take an immersion blender and blend well until you have a smooth texture.
4. Season with a bit of salt and pepper.
5. Once ready, open the lid and serve immediately.

Nutrition Values (Per Serving):

Calories: 100, Fat: 2.5g, Carbohydrates: 20g, Protein: 2g

Meal Prep Tip/Storage Advice: Once the dish is ready, let it cool and divide the dish amongst 6 individual air tight zip bags. You can store them in the fridge for 3 days and in the freezer for 3 months. When storing in the freezer, try to opt for containers that are specially designed for freezing at low temperatures to avoid freezer burn. Stainless steel containers/ thick glass mason jars/ freezer zip bags are good options. Re-heat the meal in your microwave for 3 minutes before serving.

Just Trimmed Artichokes

Serving: 3 / Prep Time: 10 minutes / Cook Time: 3 hours 30 minutes

Ingredients:

- 1 cup water
- 2 medium artichokes, trimmed
- 1 tablespoon lemon juice
- Salt to taste

Directions:

1. Add water, artichokes, lemon juice, salt to your Crock Pot Slow Cooker. Stir to coat the artichokes well.
2. Place the lid and cook on LOW for 3 hours and 30 minutes.
3. Once ready, open the lid and serve immediately.

Nutrition Values (Per Serving):

Calories: 100, Fat: 2g, Carbohydrates: 10g, Protein: 4g

Meal Prep Tip/Storage Advice: Once the meal is cooked, let it cool and divide among 3 individual air tight containers. Store the meal in the fridge for 3 days and in your freezer for 3 months.

Satisfying Green Bean Mix

Serving: 2 / Prep Time: 10 minutes / Cook Time: 2 hours

Ingredients:

- 4 cups green beans, trimmed
- 2 tablespoons butter, melted
- 2 tablespoons brown sugar
- Salt and pepper to taste
- ¼ teaspoon soy sauce

Directions:

1. Add the green beans, butter, brown sugar, salt, pepper and soy sauce to your Crock Pot Slow Cooker.
2. Toss well and place the lid. Cook on LOW for 2 hours.
3. Once ready, open the lid and serve immediately.

Nutrition Values (Per Serving):

Calories: 236, Fat: 6g, Carbohydrates: 10g, Protein: 6g

Meal Prep Tip/Storage Advice: Once the meal is cooked, let it cool and divide among 2 individual air tight containers. Store the meal in the fridge for 3 days and in your freezer for 3 months.

Crispy Peach Crumble

Serving: 4 / Prep Time: 10 minutes / Cook Time: 3 hours

Ingredients:

- 6 cups peaches, sliced
- 2 cups dried fruits and granola mix

Directions:

1. Grease the inner pot of your Slow Cooker with cooking spray.
2. Spread the peaches at the bottom. Scatter granola and nuts on top.
3. Lay a dish towel between the slow cooker and the lid.
4. Place the lid and cook on LOW for 3 hours or until the juices the bubbling. Once ready, open the lid and serve warm.

Nutrition Values (Per Serving):

Calories: 180, Fat: 2g, Carbohydrates: 39g, Protein: 5g

Meal Prep Tip/Storage Advice: Once the meal is cooked and ready, let it cool and store in 4 individual air tight containers based on the serving. The dessert can be stored in the fridge for 3 days.

Garlic And Cauliflower Mash

Serving: 4 / Prep Time: 5 minutes / Cook Time: 9 hours

Ingredients:

- 1 large cauliflower head, broke into florets
- 6 garlic cloves, peeled
- 2 tablespoons herbs, minced
- 1 cup vegetable broth
- 6 cups water
- 3 tablespoons clarified butter
- Salt to taste

Directions:

1. Peel off the leaves of the cauliflower and cut them into medium florets.
2. Add them to your slow cooker and top with garlic cloves, veggie broth and just enough water to cover the cauliflower.
3. Cook on LOW for 6 hours and then on HIGH for 3 hours.
4. Once ready, rain the water and broth and add the cauliflower back to the cooker.
5. Add butter and use immersion blender to mash them.
6. Season with salt and pepper, and sprinkle with herbs.
7. Once ready, open the lid and serve immediately.

Nutrition Values (Per Serving):

Calories: 25, Fat: 5g, Carbohydrates: 0g, Protein: 2g

Meal Prep Tip/Storage Advice: Once the meal is cooked, let it cool and divide among 4 individual air tight containers. Store the meal in the fridge for 3 days and in your freezer for 3 months. If you want to avoid freezer burn, try storing them in the freezer proof containers such as stainless steels container. Re-heat in microwave for 5 minutes before serving.

Black Eyed Peas And Spinach Platter

Serving: 4 / Prep Time: 10 minutes / Cook Time: 8 hours

Ingredients:

- 1 cup black eyed peas, soaked overnight and drained
- 2 cups low-sodium chicken broth
- 1 can (15 ounces) tomatoes, diced with juice
- 8 ounces ham, chopped
- 1 onion, chopped
- 2 garlic cloves, minced
- 1 teaspoon dried oregano
- 1 teaspoon salt
- ½ teaspoon freshly ground black pepper
- ½ teaspoon ground mustard
- 1 bay leaf

Directions:

1. Add the above listed ingredients to your Crock Pot Slow Cooker and stir well.
2. Place the lid and cook on LOW for 8 hours.
3. Once ready, discard the bay leaf and serve hot.

Nutrition Values (Per Serving):

Calories: 209, Fat: 6g, Carbohydrates: 22g, Protein: 17g

Meal Prep Tip/Storage Advice: Once the meal is cooked, let it cool and divide among 4 individual air tight containers. Store the meal in the fridge for 3 days and in your freezer for 3 months. If you want to avoid freezer burn, try storing them in the freezer proof containers such as stainless steels container. Re-heat in microwave for 5 minutes before serving.

Humble Mushroom Rice

Serving: 3 / Prep Time: 10 minutes / Cook Time: 3 hours

Ingredients:

- ½ cup rice
- 2 green onions chopped
- 1 garlic clove, minced
- ¼ pound baby Portobello mushrooms, sliced
- 1 cup beef stock

Directions:

1. Add the rice, onions, garlic, mushrooms, stock to your Crock Pot Slow Cooker.
2. Stir well and place the lid.
3. Cook on LOW for 3 hours.
4. Once ready, open the lid and stir well.
5. Divide among individual serving platters and serve.

Nutrition Values (Per Serving):

Calories: 200, Fat: 6g, Carbohydrates: 28g, Protein: 5g

Meal Prep Tip/Storage Advice: Once the meal is cooked, let it cool and divide among 3 individual air tight containers. Store the meal in the fridge for 3 days and in your freezer for 3 months. If you want to avoid freezer burn, try storing them in the freezer proof containers such as stainless steels container. Re-heat in microwave for 5 minutes before serving.

Ginger Sweet Potato Mash

Serving: 10 / Prep Time: 10 minutes / Cook Time: 3 hours

Ingredients:

- 2 ½ pounds sweet potatoes, peeled and quartered
- 1 cup water
- 1 tablespoon fresh ginger, grated
- ½ teaspoon ginger, minced
- ½ tablespoon coconut oil

Directions:

1. Add the potatoes, water and ginger to your Crock Pot Slow Cooker. Stir well.
2. Cover and cook on HIGH for 3 hours, or until the potatoes are tender.
3. Once ready, open the lid and add ghee.
4. Mash them and serve immediately.

Nutrition Values (Per Serving):

Calories: 100, Fat: 0.5g, Carbohydrates: 23g, Protein: 2g

Meal Prep Tip/Storage Advice: Once the meal is cooked, let it cool and divide among 10 individual air tight zip bags based on your serving portions. Store the meal in the fridge for 3 days and in your freezer for 3 months. If you want to avoid freezer burn, try storing them in the freezer proof containers such as stainless steels container. Re-heat in microwave for 5 minutes before serving.

Delicious Aloo Palak

Serving: 6 / Prep Time: 10 minutes / Cook Time: 6-8 hours

Ingredients:

- 2 pounds red potatoes, chopped
- 1 small onion, diced
- 1 red bell pepper, seeded and diced
- ¼ cup fresh cilantro, chopped
- ⅓ cup low-sodium veggie broth
- 1 teaspoon salt
- ½ teaspoon Garam masala
- ½ teaspoon ground cumin
- ¼ teaspoon ground turmeric
- ¼ teaspoon ground coriander
- ¼ teaspoon freshly ground black pepper
- 2 pounds fresh spinach, chopped

Directions:

1. Add the potatoes, bell pepper, onion, cilantro, broth and seasoning to your Slow Cooker. Mix well.
2. Place the spinach on top.
3. Cover with the lid and cook on LOW for 6-8 hours.
4. Once ready, open the lid and stir well. Serve and enjoy!

Nutrition Values (Per Serving):

Calories: 205, Fat: 1g, Carbohydrates: 44g, Protein: 9g

Meal Prep Tip/Storage Advice: Once the meal is cooked, let it cool and divide among 6 individual air tight containers. Store the meal in the fridge for 3 days and in your freezer for 3 months. If you want to avoid freezer burn, try storing them in the freezer proof containers such as stainless steels container. Re-heat in microwave for 5 minutes before serving.

DESSERT

Fantastic Poached Pears

Serving: 4 / Prep Time: 10 minutes / Cook Time: 5 hours

Ingredients:

- 4 pears, peeled, cored and halved
- ½ cup apple juice
- ½ cup honey
- ½ teaspoon vanilla extract
- ½ teaspoon lemon zest, grated
- 2 teaspoons ground cinnamon
- ½ teaspoon ginger, ground

Directions:

1. Place the pear halves in your Slow Cooker, with the cut side facing up.
2. Take a small bowl and add apple juice, vanilla, honey, lemon zest, cinnamon and ginger.
3. Pour the mixture over the pears.
4. Place the lid and cook on LOW for 5 hours.
5. Once ready, open the lid and serve warm.

Nutrition Values (Per Serving):

Calories: 205, Fat: 0g, Carbohydrates: 54g, Protein: 1g

Meal Prep Tip/Storage Advice: Once the meal is cooked and ready, let it cool and store in 4 individual air tight containers based on the serving. The dessert can be stored in the fridge for 3 days. Re-heat it for 3 minutes in microwave before serving. Freezing is not recommended and you should eat it as soon as possible.

Cinnamon Apple Delight

Serving: 4 / Prep Time: 10 minutes / Cook Time: 6 hours

Ingredients:

- 6 apples, cored and thinly sliced
- 1 cup honey
- 1 tablespoon ground cinnamon
- 3 tablespoons arrowroot
- Salt to taste

Directions:

1. Add the above listed ingredients to your Crock Pot Slow Cooker.
2. Stir and mix well. Cover with the lid and cook on LOW for 6 hours.
3. Once ready, open the lid and stir. Serve warm and enjoy!

Nutrition Values (Per Serving):

Calories: 306, Fat: 0g, Carbohydrates: 82g, Protein: 1g

Meal Prep Tip/Storage Advice: Once the meal is cooked and ready, let it cool and store in 4 individual air tight containers based on the serving. The dessert can be stored in the fridge for 3 days.

Hungry Hippo Rice Pudding

Serving: 4 / Prep Time: 5 minutes / Cook Time: 4 hours

Ingredients:

- ¾ cup long-grain rice
- 3 cups unsweetened almond milk
- ¾ cup honey
- 1 tablespoon ghee
- 1 teaspoon vanilla extract
- ½ teaspoon ground cinnamon
- ¼ teaspoon salt

Directions:

1. Grease with ghee the inner pot of your Slow Cooker.
2. Add in the above listed ingredients and give it a good stir.
3. Place the lid and cook on LOW for 4 hours.
4. Once ready, open the lid and serve warm.

Nutrition Values (Per Serving):

Calories: 416, Fat: 8g, Carbohydrates: 82g, Protein: 2g

Meal Prep Tip/Storage Advice: Once the meal is cooked and ready, let it cool and store in 4 individual air tight containers based on the serving. The dessert can be stored in the fridge for 3 days.

Lovely Pumpkin Pie Oats

Serving: 7 / Prep Time: 5 minutes / Cook Time: 8-9 hours

Ingredients:

- 2 cups uncooked steel cut oats
- 8 cups unsweetened almond milk
- 1 can (15 ounces) pumpkin puree
- 1 ½ tablespoons pumpkin pie spice
- ⅓ cup brown sugar
- 1 cup unsalted pecans, chopped

Directions:

1. Add the oats, pumpkin puree, almond milk, pumpkin pie spice, cinnamon, brown sugar to your Crock Pot Slow Cooker.
2. Stir and place the lid. Cook on LOW for 8-9 hours.
3. Once ready, open the lid and serve topped with pecans.

Nutrition Values (Per Serving):

Calories: 395, Fat: 18g, Carbohydrates: 58g, Protein: 12g

Meal Prep Tip/Storage Advice: Once the porridge if cooked let it cool and divide the servings amongst 7 individual air tight zip bags. Store them in the fridge for 6 days or in your freezer for 6 months.

Exquisite Banana Bread

Serving: 6 / Prep Time: 12 minutes / Cook Time: 3 hours

Ingredients:

- ½ cup ghee, melted
- 2 large eggs
- ½ cup honey
- 1 teaspoon baking powder
- ½ teaspoon salt
- 2 ½ cups almond flour
- ½ teaspoon baking soda
- 4 ripe bananas, mashed

Directions:

1. Coat generously the inner pot of your Crock Pot Slow Cooker.
2. Take a large bowl and whisk in the ghee, honey, eggs, baking powder, baking soda, salt and mix well.
3. Stir in the almond flour and mashed bananas.
4. Pour the batter into your Slow Cooker.
5. Lay a dish towel between the lid and the cooker's top.
6. Cover with the lid and cook on LOW for 3 hours.
7. Once ready, open the lid and serve immediately.

Nutrition Values (Per Serving):

Calories: 327, Fat: 17g, Carbohydrates: 44g, Protein: 6g

Meal Prep Tip/Storage Advice: Once the cake is baked, let it cool and slice. Transfer the slices to a large air tight container and store in the fridge for up to 7 days. Alternatively, if you want to store in the freezer, wrap the baked cake in aluminum foil and place in stainless steel container or freezer safe zip bag. Can be stored for 3 months. Re-heat in microwave for 3 minutes before serving.

Orange Sweet Potatoes

Serving: 3 / Prep Time: 10 minutes / Cook Time: 3 hours

Ingredients:

- ½ pound sweet potatoes, thinly sliced
- ½ tablespoon sugar
- 2 tablespoons orange juice
- 1 pinch of salt and pepper
- ¼ teaspoon thyme, dried
- ¼ teaspoon sage, dried
- ½ tablespoon olive oil

Directions:

1. Arrange the potato slices into your Crock Pot Slow Cooker's inner pot.
2. Take a bowl and whisk in the orange juice, salt, pepper, sugar, thyme, oil, sage.
3. Pour the mixture over potatoes.
4. Place the lid and cook on HIGH for 3 hours.
5. Once ready, open the lid and serve immediately.

Nutrition Values (Per Serving):

Calories: 189, Fat: 4g, Carbohydrates: 17g, Protein: 4g

Meal Prep Tip/Storage Advice: Once the meal is cooked and ready, let it cool and store in 3 individual air tight containers based on the serving. The dessert can be stored in the fridge for 3 days. Re-heat it for 3 minutes in microwave before serving. Freezing is not recommended and you should eat it as soon as possible.

Apricot And Ginger Brown Rice Pudding

Serving: 4 / Prep Time: 10 minutes / Cook Time: 6 hours

Ingredients:

- 3 ½ cups low fat milk
- ⅔ cup brown rice
- ⅔ cup unsweetened dried apricots, chopped
- ¼ cup honey
- 1 teaspoon ground ginger
- 1 teaspoon pure vanilla extract

Directions:

1. Add the above listed ingredients to your Slow Cooker.
2. Place the lid and cook on LOW for 6 hours or until the pudding is thick.
3. Add a bit of milk if the pudding becomes too thick.
4. Serve warm or chilled depending on your preference.

Nutrition Values (Per Serving):

Calories: 256, Fat: 2g, Carbohydrates: 53g, Protein: 8g

Meal Prep Tip/Storage Advice: Once the meal is cooked and ready, let it cool and store in 4 individual air tight containers based on the serving. The dessert can be stored in the fridge for 3 days. Re-heat it for 3 minutes in microwave before serving. Freezing is not recommended and you should eat it as soon as possible.

A HANDFUL OF KITCHEN STAPLES

Premium Marinara Sauce

Serving: 12 / Prep Time: 5 minutes / Cook Time: 8 hours

Ingredients:

- 6 pounds Roma tomatoes, chopped
- 1 can (6 ounce) tomato paste
- 6 garlic cloves, minced
- 1 large onion, finely chopped
- 1 medium red bell pepper, chopped
- 1 medium carrot, shredded
- 2 teaspoons dried basils
- 1 teaspoon dried oregano
- ½ teaspoon dried thyme
- ½ teaspoon dried marjoram
- ½ teaspoon crushed red pepper flakes

Directions:

1. Add the above listed ingredients to your Slow Cooker, and stir well.
2. Cover with the lid and cook on LOW for 8 hours.
3. Once ready, open the lid and using an immersion blender, crush the tomatoes to your desired consistency.
4. Serve as desired.

Nutrition Values (Per Serving):

Calories: 71, Fat: 0g, Carbohydrates: 16g, Protein: 3g

Meal Prep Tip/Storage Advice: Once the sauce is cooked, let it cool and transfer to air tight (thick glassed) mason jars, store in the fridge for 3 days.

Spicy- Any Time Apple Sauce

Serving: 8 / Prep Time: 8 minutes / Cook Time: 4 hours

Ingredients:

- 5 pounds apples, peeled, cored and quartered
- Juice of 1 lemon
- 2 teaspoons ground cinnamon
- ½ teaspoon ground nutmeg
- ¼ teaspoon ground cloves
- ¼ teaspoon ground ginger

Directions:

1. Add the above listed ingredients to your Slow Cooker.
2. Place the lid and cook on HIGH for 4 hours.
3. Once ready, open the lid and mash the contents using a potato masher.
4. Serve warm and enjoy!

Nutrition Values (Per Serving):

Calories: 140, Fat: 0g, Carbohydrates: 3g, Protein: 1g

Meal Prep Tip/Storage Advice: Once the sauce is cooked, let it cool and transfer to air tight (thick glassed) mason jars, store in the fridge for 3 days. If you want to store in the freezer, you may transfer the sauce to freezer safe zip bags and store in the freezer for 6 months. Re-heat in your microwave for 3 minutes and use immediately.

Vegan Alfredo Sauce

Serving: 4 / Prep Time: 5 minutes / Cook Time: 8 hours

Ingredients:

- 3 cups vegetable broth
- 1 cup raw cashews
- 1 cup water
- ½ cup unsweetened soymilk
- ½ cup nutritional yeast
- 1 teaspoon dried mustard
- Juice of ½ lemon
- Pinch of salt

Directions:

1. Add the above listed ingredients to your Slow Cooker.
2. Place the lid and cook on LOW for 8 hours.
3. Once ready, open the lid and puree using immersion blender.
4. Serve warm.

Nutrition Values (Per Serving):

Calories: 133, Fat: 9g, Carbohydrates: 10g, Protein: 8g

Meal Prep Tip/Storage Advice: Once the sauce is cooked, let it cool and transfer to air tight (thick glassed) mason jars, store in the fridge for 3 days. If you want to store in the freezer, you may transfer the sauce to freezer safe zip bags and store in the freezer for 6 months. Re-heat in your microwave for 3 minutes and use immediately.

Inspiring Home-Made Ketchup

Serving: 4 / Prep Time: 5 minutes / Cook Time: 8 hours

Ingredients:

- 4 pounds tomatoes, seeded and chopped
- ⅔ cup apple cider vinegar
- ½ cup onion, chopped
- ¼ cup brown sugar
- 1 teaspoon smoked paprika
- 1 teaspoon garlic powder
- ½ teaspoon celery seed
- ½ teaspoon freshly ground black pepper
- ½ teaspoon salt
- ⅛ teaspoon ground mustard powder

Directions:

1. Add the above listed ingredients to your Slow Cooker.
2. Place the lid and cook on LOW for 8 hours or until the ketchup has reduced and thickened.
3. Once ready, open the lid and use an immersion blender to puree the ketchup. Use as needed.

Nutrition Values (Per Serving):

Calories: 23, Fat: 0g, Carbohydrates: 6g, Protein: 1g

Meal Prep Tip/Storage Advice: Once the sauce is cooked, let it cool and transfer to air tight (thick glassed) mason jars, store in the fridge for 3 days. If you want to store in the freezer, you may transfer the sauce to freezer safe zip bags and store in the freezer for 6 months. Re-heat in your microwave for 3 minutes and use immediately.

Orange And Chili Garlic Sauce

Serving: 5 cups / Prep Time: 15 minutes / Cook Time: 8 hours

Ingredients:

- ½ cup apple cider vinegar
- 4 pounds red jalapeno peppers, stems, seeds and ribs removed, chopped
- 10 garlic cloves, chopped
- ½ cup tomato paste
- Juice of 1 orange zest
- ½ cup honey
- 2 tablespoons soy sauce
- 2 teaspoons salt

Directions:

1. Add the vinegar, garlic, peppers, tomato paste, orange juice, honey, zest, soy sauce and salt to your Slow Cooker.
2. Stir well and close the lid.
3. Cook on LOW for 8 hours.
4. Once ready, open the lid and let cool.
5. Use as needed.

Nutrition Values (Per Serving):

Calories: 33, Fat: 1g, Carbohydrates: 8g, Protein: 1g

Meal Prep Tip/Storage Advice: Once the sauce is cooked, let it cool and transfer to air tight (thick glassed) mason jars, store in the fridge for 3 days. If you want to store in the freezer, you may transfer the sauce to freezer safe zip bags and store in the freezer for 6 months. Re-heat in your microwave for 3 minutes and use immediately.

Creamiest Cheese Dip Ever!

Serving: 12 / Prep Time: 5 minutes / Cook Time: 4 hours

Ingredients:

- 1 bag (12 ounces0 frozen pureed butternut squash, thawed
- 8 ounces low fat pepper jack cheese, cut into cubes
- 8 ounces low fat cream cheese
- 1 can (4 and ½ ounces) green chilies, chopped
- 2 scallions, thinly sliced
- ½ cup 1% milk
- ½ teaspoon garlic powder
- Fresh cilantro, garnish (optional)

Directions:

1. Add the above listed ingredients, except for the cilantro, to your Slow Cooker.
2. Place the lid and cook on LOW for 4 hours or until all Ingredients are melt smoothly.
3. Serve warm and garnish with freshly chopped cilantro (if desired).

Nutrition Values (Per Serving):

Calories: 109, Fat: 6g, Carbohydrates: 6g, Protein: 6g

Meal Prep Tip/Storage Advice: Once the sauce is cooked, let it cool and transfer to air tight (thick glassed) mason jars, store in the fridge for 3 days. If you want to store in the freezer, you may transfer the sauce to freezer safe zip bags and store in the freezer for 6 months. Re-heat in your microwave for 3 minutes and use immediately.

Homemade Cranberry Sauce

Serving: 1 and ½ cups / Prep Time: 5 minutes / Cook Time: 8 hours

Ingredients:

- 12 ounces fresh cranberries
- ½ cup 100% orange juice
- ½ cup water
- ½ cup sugar
- Ground ginger, cinnamon, clove, vanilla extract (optional to taste)

Directions:

1. Add the above listed Ingredients to your Slow Cooker.
2. Place the lid and cook on LOW for 8 hours until the cranberries have popped open.
3. Taste the sauce and stir in extra sweetener or garnish if needed.

Nutrition Values (Per Serving):

Calories: 155, Fat: 0g, Carbohydrates: 40g, Protein: 1g

Meal Prep Tip/Storage Advice: Once the sauce is cooked, let it cool and transfer to air tight (thick glassed) mason jars, store in the fridge for 3 days. If you want to store in the freezer, you may transfer the sauce to freezer safe zip bags and store in the freezer for 6 months. Re-heat in your microwave for 3 minutes and use immediately.

Tantalizing Mushroom Gravy

Serving: 2 cups / Prep Time: 5 minutes / Cook Time: 6 hours

Ingredients:

- 1 cup button mushrooms, sliced
- ¾ cup low-fat buttermilk
- ⅓ cup water
- 1 medium onion, finely diced
- 2 garlic cloves, minced
- 2 tablespoons extra virgin olive oil
- 2 tablespoons all-purpose flour
- 1 tablespoon fresh rosemary, minced
- Freshly ground black pepper

Directions:

1. Add the above listed Ingredients to your Crock Pot Slow Cooker.
2. Place the lid and cook on LOW for 6 hours.
3. Serve warm and use as desired.

Nutrition Values (Per Serving):

Calories: 54, Fat: 4g, Carbohydrates: 4g, Protein: 2g

Meal Prep Tip/Storage Advice: Once the sauce is cooked, let it cool and transfer to air tight (thick glassed) mason jars, store in the fridge for 3 days. If you want to store in the freezer, you may transfer the sauce to freezer safe zip bags and store in the freezer for 6 months. Re-heat in your microwave for 3 minutes and use immediately.

All-Purpose Bone Broth

Serving: 10 cups / Prep Time: 5 minutes / Cook Time: 12-24/ 24-48 hours

Ingredients:

- 3 pounds poultry, pork, lamb or beef broth
- 1 garlic head, unpeeled, halved across middle
- 1 onion, unpeeled, quartered pole to pole
- 2 carrots, unpeeled and halved
- 2 celery stalks, unpeeled and halved
- 1 tablespoons apple cider vinegar
- 2 dried bay leaves
- 2 fresh rosemary sprigs
- 2 fresh thyme sprigs
- 10 peppercorns
- ½ teaspoon salt
- Enough water to fill ¾ of the Slow Cooker

Directions:

1. Add the bones, onions, garlic, celery, carrots, vinegar, bay leaves, thyme, rosemary, peppercorns, salt and water to your Slow Cooker.
2. Close the lid and cook on LOW for 12-24 hours (if poultry) and 24-48 hours (if pork, lamb or beef bones).
3. Strain the liquid through a cloth mesh or metal mesh.
4. Discard solids and use as needed.

Nutrition Values (Per Serving):

Calories: 38, Fat: 5g, Carbohydrates: 1g, Protein: 5g

Meal Prep Tip/Storage Advice: Can be kept in air tight containers in the fridge for up to 2 weeks, and in the freezer for up to 2 months.

Everyday Vegetable Stock

Serving: 10 cups / Prep Time: 5 minutes / Cook Time: 8-10 hours

Ingredients:

- 2 celery stalks (with leaves), quartered
- 4 ounces mushrooms, with stems
- 2 carrots, unpeeled and quartered
- 1 onion, unpeeled, quartered from pole to pole
- 1 garlic head, unpeeled, halved across middle
- 2 fresh thyme sprigs
- 10 peppercorns
- ½ teaspoon salt
- Enough water to fill 3 quarters of Slow Cooker

Directions:

1. Add celery, mushrooms, onion, carrots, garlic, thyme, salt, peppercorn and water to your Slow Cooker.
2. Stir and cover with the lid.
3. Cook on LOW for 8-10 hours.
4. Strain the stock through a fine mesh cloth/metal mesh and discard solids.
5. Use as needed.

Nutrition Values (Per Serving):

Calories: 38, Fat: 5g, Carbohydrates: 1g, Protein: 0g

Meal Prep Tip/Storage Advice: Can be kept in air tight containers in the fridge for up to 2 weeks, and in the freezer for up to 2 months.

CPSIA information can be obtained
at www.ICGtesting.com
Printed in the USA
LVHW05s1635131018
593395LV00002BA/2/P